641.86 MCK

STICKY FINGERS

GREEN THUMB

Sticky Fingers, Green Thumb

Baked sweets that taste of nature

Hayley McKee

hardie grant books

Cakes 61

Sweet snacks 115

I love digging my hands into butter and sugar just as much as groping around in the earth. For me, baking and gardening are inseparable; but I took the long way home to make this connection.

I started Sticky Fingers Bakery when the cupcake craze hit the world. A self-taught baker, I threw myself in the deep end, baking tiny cakes full of punchy attitude and big flavours. Blending traditional baked goods with offbeat ingredients made my menus a bit of a hit around town and as my client list grew so did the scale and scope of my cakes.

Even though there was magic to these decorated cakes – piled high with fluorescent, store-bought ingredients – this style of baking never really satisfied me. I wanted to hunt down wholesome, unconventional flavours far away from the supermarket shelves.

A breakthrough came when I realised that everything else I ate, and everything I believed in about good food, was based around real ingredients. I cared about where I shopped, the produce I bought and who I bought it from, but my cakes lacked this connection to local suppliers and natural ingredients. My baking shifted when I switched on to local growers' and farmers' markets and, most importantly, to edible gardens.

By tuning into the plant world I eventually arrived where I belonged: baking sweets that tasted of nature. Where the ingredients were familiar, the colourings genuine and the flavours unmasked. Vegetables, herbs and edible flowers gave me vivid flavours to explore and offered a savoury–sweet balance that satisfied without overwhelming. Soulful, earthy and seasonal baking became my true direction and, ultimately, my signature style.

A baker's garden

I'm a more skilful baker than I am a gardener, but you'll always find edibles sprouting around my home and in my community garden plot.

Rosemary, basil, thyme, calendula, nasturtium, tomato, rocket and scented geraniums are my trusted staples and are always within arms' reach of my kitchen. These are the green ones I fold into my baking time and again. I enjoy watching for plants to sprout and be ripe for the picking, and I like that my recipes lie ready for the right season to come – waiting for my garden produce to be at its peak before it's combined with the creamiest of butters, free-range eggs and a little something sweet.

Growing your own food isn't a new concept, obviously. But in recent years it's re-emerged as an important feature of cooking with a conscience. More and more of us are sensitive to the origins of our food. We're savvier to the mysteries of mass-processed foods and supermarket monopolies, and this has led to an openhearted attempt to grow our own produce again, however humble our space.

We're relearning something that has always been intuitive to us.

For me, baking is a beautiful solo experience, while gardening is a more collective activity, and I've learned a lot about the produce I bake with thanks largely to my talented friends, family and neighbours who expertly maintain their kitchen gardens with skill and devotion. They are my horticultural hotlines. The same goes for my community garden – their workshops and events nurture sustainability and a sense of place, and volunteering there gives me a beautiful slice of back-to-basics living that I'm able to feed right back into the spirit of my recipes.

It's these links to the environment and the earth that are so important to both my baking and my overall wellbeing. The sensory experiences of being in the kitchen and the garden have become my creative outlet and my escape into the slow lane.

Outdoors indoors: this book's job

These recipes make you think about being outside. As you prepare each garden ingredient, let it pull your imagination out of the kitchen window and into the bigger picture, of seasons and locality.

Count on these recipes for desserts and snacks with a neighbourhood-bake feel that celebrates real garden produce.

These grown ingredients haven't been included just to be quirky – this book isn't about shock value. It's about turning a spotlight on underestimated and underused produce and cherishing what unique flavours can be brought to the dessert table. I don't want to mask the organic beauty of the outdoors. I want to incorporate it into really good baked desserts that acknowledge their taste and where they come from (hopefully, your backyard).

Alongside most recipes – whether for cakes, tarts, cookies, brownies or muffins – you'll find gardening tips on how to grow the key ingredients in your own baker's garden. It doesn't matter if that garden is a little windowsill of herbs or one big unruly planter of vegetables; if every time you pluck your home-grown produce you think about a sweet use for it, then this book has done its job.

For me, cakes and sweets shouldn't be 'skinnyfied', so this isn't about using garden greenery for healthy baking. Although most of my recipes happen to be lean on sugar, that's only because I prefer the hero ingredients to shine. Other than that, I use good butter, full-fat milk and nearly always add a dollop of cream on the side. Baked desserts are treats, not staples. Eat everything in moderation, but celebrate the good times with something gooey and mouth-watering from your oven. You deserve it.

Be free

BE IMAGINATIVE AND EXPERIMENT.
Don't be afraid to substitute ingredients
to make these creations your own. Play
around with quantities to dial up or down
the flavours you prefer. Trust yourself,
and your tastebuds.

BAKE WITH A SENSE OF HUMOUR.
Things can go wrong in the world
of baking. Embrace and own these
happy accidents and approach
these recipes with a sense of
adventure and a relaxed attitude.

GROWING YOUR OWN PRODUCE WILL MAKE
YOU CHERISH EACH MOUTHFUL EVEN MORE.
But if it can't be garden-fresh,
don't beat yourself up. You can
still add meaning to your desserts
by picking the best produce you
can afford and trying to connect
with your local suppliers.

REMEMBER THAT PLANTS
GROW ON THEIR OWN CYCLE.
This book's garden tidbits will help
them along, but you shouldn't give
up if there are plantings that fail.
Just keep nurturing them, and your
green thumb, as best you can.

BE GENEROUS.
Don't count calories
or think about using
skim milk instead of
full-cream milk. Make
these baked goods
your ultimate treat.
Make them to impress.

Vegetables

Vegetables are particularly versatile in baking, yet are so often forgotten. They offer a broad scale of flavours, provide form, add moisture and create texture. Root vegetables crop up in cakes, with carrots, pumpkins and beetroots being the most loved and well known, but turning to your salad bowl for inspiration can provide even more flavour ideas.

My most-loved vegetables add earthiness and a hint of nature to cakes, cookies, slices and pies. There are other vegetables that I'm sure are compatible with baking but, for me, if they don't hit the flavour mark then they've not been included (I'm looking at you, cauliflower). Just because you can find a clever way to incorporate a vegetable into a dessert, doesn't mean you should.

So, when it comes time to pluck your veggies from your garden (or a local farmers' market), instead of turning to the same savoury classics, try exploring this alternative collection of recipes made especially for your sweet tooth. For instance, say goodbye to your annual flood of zucchini fritters and hello to coffee, banana and zucchini loaf (page 68).

Flavour notes

Some of the vegetables in this section are technically fruits but, because their taste and use are generally more associated with the vegetable family, I've kept them in the gang.

AVOCADO

With the texture of butter and the taste of fresh, grassy cream, avocados make an easy leap into baked sweets. Incorporate them into buttercreams or to give soft body to batters and doughs. Their delicate, fatty base notes work equally well with bright acidic flavours or oaky, dark chocolate. As an aside, their cool lusciousness makes them a good ally for mousses, ice creams and no-bake pie fillings.

BEETROOT (BEET)

Whether used roasted, steamed or raw, dense, crimson beetroot adds a unique taste lying somewhere between a deep, robust funk and a sweet, floral perfume. Baby beetroots are more manageable to work with and roasting them is the least messy mode of preparation. Use golden beetroots or the candy-striped Chioggia variety for eye-catching garnishes, and use the juice as a natural food dye.

CARROT

Sweet, juicy carrots are the most classic of cake buddies. They belong to the same flowering plant family as celery and parsley, which you can taste hints of when you eat them raw. Use heirloom carrots for their rainbow colours of red, white, yellow and purple.

CHERRY TOMATO

Vine-ripened cherry tomatoes, warmed by the sun, are the reward that every home gardener savours. Leafy, acidic and jammy in flavour, tomatoes can be reminiscent of strawberries, so substituting them in your favourite berry recipes makes a great starting point.

EGGPLANT (AUBERGINE)

Eggplant is sublimely buttery when roasted and makes an excellent vehicle for absorbing other flavours. Always soak your eggplants in cold, salted water to draw out any hidden bitterness.

FENNEL

I am a sucker for this plant. Sweet anise perfume gives it an unmatched flavour. From bulb to fronds you can eat all parts, including the seeds and pollen. The liquorice tones of the bulb can be very subtle; for more of a kick, use ground or whole fennel seeds.

GREEN LEAVES

Spinach, kale and rocket (arugula) are my go-to greens in baking. Mostly I use them to add a whisper of colour, but kale crisps can add a nice crunch to desserts, while a smidgen of rocket can be an interesting bridge between sugar and spice.

MUSHROOM

There are only a few mushrooms suitable for sweets; the earthy, chocolate depth of porcini make them my favourite, though shiitake and pine mushrooms can bring a creamy, woodland element too. Because of mushroom's intensely concentrated flavours, sliced and dried are better than fresh.

PARSNIP

Parsnips should be every baker's friend – they have similar fruity tones to bananas and apples and their spicy complexity gives a suggestion of nutmeg, coriander (cilantro) and parsley.

PEA

This rambling, tiny veg can bring a pop of grassy freshness to creams and custards. Steamed and then blended, pea purée is the best way to infuse baked goods with the taste of spring.

POTATO

Don't overthink it, just incorporate them as they're best loved – either as a fluffy, creamy mash or crisped up and salted. Faintly buttery and sweet, spuds add earthy depth and moisture to cakes or a fun crunch to cookies and crusts.

PUMPKIN (WINTER SQUASH)

Ninety per cent water, pumpkins can be turned to for an injection of rich moisture. There's a fruitiness to them that mimics rockmelon (netted melon/canteloupe), and they have an amazing ability to delicately colour buttercreams and fillings.

RHUBARB

Tart, herbaceous rhubarb has long been associated with winter puddings and crumbles, and rightly so. With its citrus-like punch and suggestion of rose petals, this is a beautiful vegetable to pair with nuggets of dark chocolate and lashings of whipped cream.

SWEETCORN

Except in Latin American cuisine, sweetcorn is an underused companion for desserts. Include the juicy, starchy kernels as a base for custards and pastry creams, or experiment with golden sweetcorn juice as a milk substitute in recipes.

SWEET POTATO

Brown butter and honeycomb come to mind when I think of these burnt orange roots. There's a light nuttiness to this vegetable that makes it a dream to create recipes with. Just like pumpkin, it brings a silky finish to cake batters.

ZUCCHINI (COURGETTE)

Because of its watery texture, zucchini needs support when baked. Squeezing the liquid out of it is the secret. Once drained, it will inject whatever you are making with lots of moisture and a mild, cucumber-like flavour.

If you can't grow it, then buy the best produce you can.

Techniques and methods

ROAST

Roasting vegetables to a creamy consistency is the best method for drawing out their true, rounded flavours. Adding a dash of olive oil or butter to the roasting pan is fine, just remember to hold the salt.

STEAM

When you're poor on time, skip the roasting and steam your veg instead. Steaming keeps the form and colour of vegetables intact far better than boiling them.

JUICE

Brilliantly coloured vegetable juice is great to use as a natural food dye, a liquid substitute in recipes or a shrubby base for syrups and caramels.

INFUSE

Give pastry creams and custards a blast from the garden by gently simmering the milk with grated vegetables. Strain before use.

PURÉE

Blitz your cooked vegetables to a purée and strain them through a sieve to remove excess moisture or lumps. Swirl the purée into batters or freshly whipped cream, or pipe it into the centre of muffins.

GRATE

Grated vegetables add structure and bite to desserts by delivering extra texture. For juicy vegetables, use a standard cheese grater on its coarse side. For woodier root vegetables, pick up the microplane.

PRESERVE

Bubble up a jam, make a quick pickle for some bite, or candy some micro vegetables to create an edible miniature garden topping.

Herbs and edible flowers

More than sugar and spice, I love folding herbs and flowers into my desserts to lend them a botanical, green edge. Used in subtle ratios, their mysterious undertone can be hard to pin down.

When baking with these ingredients, a little goes a long way. You don't want your cookies to taste like a conifer. You just want a modest pinch of organic seasoning.

It's particularly easy to go overboard using herbs, so the trick here is to go easy and taste, taste, taste. Some herbs can be so pungent they knock out sweetness and replace it with bitterness.

The same goes for edible flowers. Many flower varieties just bring a peppery slap to your palate but ultimately don't lend much flavour. I've chewed my way through many petals and compiled the most blossomy and satisfying bunch to bake with.

Store your fresh herbs like you would fresh-cut flowers, dipped in a glass of clean water and kept away from direct sun. If you want to prolong freshness, cover the glass with a clear plastic bag to create a mini greenhouse effect. Flowers, once plucked, should be kept in an airtight container and stored in the fridge. Don't forget to leave some flowers for the bees to help pollinate your bounty for the next bloom. You can also dry your edible flowers by hanging them upside down in a cool, dark place. Once dry, store them in an airtight container of caster sugar to help them last even longer and to inject their perfume into your granules.

Most herbs are evergreen and will last throughout the seasons, but edible flowers can be season specific. Drying them is a good way to preserve supplies, but remember the flavour will be less intense. Toast them before use to draw out their aromas.

Flavour notes – herbs

BASIL

Deeply fragrant with a murmur of aniseed, basil is a member of the mint family and one of the fruitiest herbs available. Fresh torn leaves incorporated into butter, blitzed with olive oil or rubbed through sugar will give your baked goods a brilliant green tinge and an exotic, lush roundness. Try Thai, lemon, lime, cinnamon or purple basil for a different twist.

BAY LEAF

There's a place for bay leaves other than soups and stews. Wholly herbal and with a suggestion of eucalyptus, bay leaves lend an inkling of oregano and a dry, forest air to desserts. Use them as a poaching agent or finely ground as a flavouring for batters and doughs.

CORIANDER (CILANTRO)

Jungle wet and zesty, you either love or loathe this herb. Coriander's floral accents can often taste soapy if used in excess. Pair it with fatty ingredients, such as avocado, nut or coconut cream, to provide contrast. When cooked, coriander leaves don't hold much colour or flavour, so using them raw is the best option. Freshly ground coriander seeds blended into cooked desserts will represent the complete flavour of coriander best.

PEPPERMINT

Personally, I loathe spearmint. Its sickly sweet taste reminds me of a bad milkshake from my teens. Peppermint is the only menthol for me. It lends freshness to bitter components, such as dark chocolate and sharp plums, and it can be a soothing partner for spicy ingredients, from chilli to nutmeg.

PINEAPPLE SAGE

Native to Central America, this bushy herb is like nature's pineapple lolly. It tastes artificial at times because the flavour is so exact and tropical. Both the leaves and flowers are edible, so it's a brilliant multi-purpose herb to have on hand.

ROSEMARY

Reminiscent of evergreen pine and smoky lavender, rosemary is a powerful flavour to play with. Pair it with sharp citrus or use it to balance out bold flavours, such as star anise. Avoid woody textures by only using the leaves fresh and finely sliced.

SAGE

Not as exciting as pineapple sage and just as intense as rosemary, sage's damp, meaty character can add depth to desserts but, because of its pronounced flavour, it should be used in modest amounts.

TARRAGON

There's a moreish taste to tarragon that I can't get enough of. The creamy anise layers add an elegant shade to sweets laced with vanilla bean or chocolate.

THYME

Bittersweet and aromatic, thyme is loved by bees. Take a cue from them and partner this herb with honey-soaked desserts. There are over twenty varieties of woody thyme but, for me, lemon, orange and juniper thyme are the softest ones to pair with baking.

Flavour notes – edible flowers

VEGETABLE FLOWERS

Parsnip, rocket, broad bean, fennel, cucumber and radish all produce edible flowers that can be teamed up with sugar. Most of these flowers take on faint flavour characteristics of the vegetable, so use that cue to select which to pair with other ingredients.

FRUIT FLOWERS

The blossoms of orange, lemon, plum, grapefruit, cherry and apple trees are sweet and simple flowers that bear the scent of the fruit trees they belong to. Their petals are meatier than those of other edible flowers, making them a good choice for crystallising and decorating.

HERB FLOWERS

These appear when herb plants 'bolt' or go to seed. During this stage of the growth cycle the leaves of your herbs grow tougher and less palatable, so you're trading off the quality of the herb for the beauty of the flower. Dill, tarragon, thyme, rosemary, lemon verbena, sage, peppermint, coriander (cilantro) and oregano all sprout pretty flowers ideal for sweet recipes. As with vegetable flowers, these buds take on the flavour characteristics of the herb.

BORAGE

Bright blue borage is a fuzzy floral with a simple, cucumber flavour. It works beautifully with berries as well as other gentle ingredients, such as avocado and dairy.

CALENDULA

Bright yellow and orange calendulas are part of the marigold family, but they more resemble large cartoon daisies. Their flavour is less rounded than marigold, but they still hold a bright, honey bend.

CHAMOMILE

Milky and sweet with honey accents, daisy-shaped chamomile has a soft flavour that matches particularly well with buttery vanilla bean bases and maple syrup.

CORNFLOWER

A pom-pom flower that adds grassy clove notes to desserts, cornflower complements warm winter aromas of cinnamon, ginger and nutmeg. Sticky dates, figs and apple pie are good companions too. An excellent natural food dye.

ELDERFLOWER

This flower smacks of an English summer. The taste is a blend of peach, pear and apple blossoms. It's most commonly used to make syrups and cordials, which make great soaking liquids for adding moisture to cakes.

SCENTED GERANIUM

Use the aromatic oil from the leaves of scented geraniums, which come in a range of delicious flavours, such as rose, orange, peppermint, coconut and clove. The flowers are less flavourful but add a simple charm as decorations.

HIBISCUS

Tart and cranberry-like, this tropical bloom adds vibrant colour and tang. I love it in jams or as a berry replacement. Anywhere a raspberry is suited, the hibiscus will be at home.

HONEYSUCKLE

A cutie-pie bloom in looks and taste. Avoid a saccharine overload and match it with toasted flavours, such as oats, almonds, brown butter and maple syrup.

JASMINE

The flavour of star-shaped jasmine is heavily fragrant with tea-like characteristics. The epitome of a hazy summer afternoon treat.

LAVENDER

Adds a musky tone to creamy components or a pretty garden twist to chocolate bases. Use in small doses.

LILAC

A lemon balm flavour with a bittersweet tinge. Lilac makes a lovely, fragrant syrup and gives a natural purple blush to desserts. Pair it with tart berries, heavy creams and earthy vegetables.

MARIGOLD

A soulful, pollen-heavy floral that Mexico regards as 'the scent of heaven'. The petals lend desserts a mild radish-like spice, a honey tinge and a saffron hue. French marigolds are the pretty ruffled varietal commonly grown in a burgundy shade with orange trims.

NASTURTIUM

Nasturtium's sweet and spicy leaves, seeds and flowers bring a grassy, fresh bite to desserts. They're a beautiful rambling decoration for cakes, with the zebra variety being particularly pretty.

ROSE

Thanks to Turkish delight and rosewater, this is the most loved and used flower in cooking. Use in small quantities to add a delicate perfume to almost any sweet staple.

SUNFLOWER

A versatile plant that gives a bold blast of yellow from the petals and a soft crunch from the seeds. Use the young buds, which taste a little like artichoke, as the older, bigger flowers tend to be bitter.

VIOLA

A traditional cake decoration but also a beautifully light and perfumed flower similar to blueberries, lemon blossom and honey. Eat the whole flower for the fullest mouthful. Pansies are the big sister of viola in looks but not taste, though they are useful for when you want to supersize your decorations.

To make sure they're safe for consumption, only pick edible flowers that have been grown organically without the use of pesticides.

Techniques and methods

CREAM

At the heart of most baked recipes is the creaming stage. Beating flowers and herbs with your butter and sugar on high speed will drum their colour and herbaceous tinge into your finished creation.

SMOKE

Dried petals and herbs are great for giving liquids or dry ingredients a smoky waft of botanicals.

INFUSE

Simmering milk with herbs or flowers adds an earthiness to baked goods and creates a complex flavour base for making custards and pastry creams. Rubbing fresh torn herbs or petals through your sugar will inject your baking staples with a raw, wild twist.

EXTRACT

Create your own flavour extracts from sweet, potent herbs, such as peppermint and lemon thyme, or punchy, fragrant flowers, such as citrus blossoms, roses and jasmine.

STEEP

Herbs or flowers steeped in vinegar, oil or honey will give these liquids a new botanical depth. The longer you let the flavours mingle, the more complex the result.

Real baking know-how

Most of what I know about cake making I learned from pizza. Throughout my school years, I worked at pizza joints and patisseries. The French pastry chefs showed me what a tightly run kitchen looked like, and the pizza chefs taught me all about flavour ratios.

My biggest lesson came from my time at Golden Pizza in the sleepy hills of Kalamunda, Western Australia. It was run by an old Italian dad. I was shown that quality toppings should be respected and arranged with care. I was taught not to skimp on the edges and to make every bite count.

Every time I create a new baked concoction I have this message in mind. Each wedge of cake, just like a good wedge of pizza, needs to have a satisfying balance of flavours – never too much of one ingredient to make it overpowering and never too little of another to make it redundant. This is the core of my baking style – flavour-packed treats that aren't loaded with empty gestures.

Cakes and other sweet treats are made with an event or someone special in mind (even if that person is you), so I really believe in stripping out the mystery and science of baking and letting it be a messy, honest experience that is fun, not stressful. I'm going to walk you through all my nuggets of know-how to help take the fear out of baking. Be bold in the kitchen and hold on to your sense of humour. Here's how.

The baker's toolkit
(spatulas matter)

Okay, first up you need to have a baker's toolkit. Nothing fancy, just the real essentials to get you baking with results. Open your kitchen drawer and survey your gadgets. If your spatula has seen better days, treat yourself to a new one. Ditto your whisk and measuring cups. As soon as you have a functioning batch of utensils you'll notice that you start baking more and more. And the more you bake, the better you get.

The following are what you need for a functioning, humble kitchen. Just like the natural ingredients I'm drawn to, nothing included here is overly pricey or fancy; these are just the core items you need to line you up for baking success.

Electric oven

I have spent many years picking rental homes purely based on their ovens. Your oven is clearly your biggest ally in baking well-risen cakes, and I always choose electric models over gas. Generally, gas ovens keep all the heat in the back and don't circulate the hot air for an even bake. If you do have a gas oven, factor in time to carefully rotate your baked goods halfway through the baking time.

Stand mixer

Buying your first stand mixer is a rite of passage for any serious home baker. It's an investment that marks your commitment and enthusiasm, and it will help you cut time and corners in whisking, kneading and beating. I use a KitchenAid stand mixer but also a Breville. The KitchenAid is a warrior and has endured years of beating monster-loads of cookie dough. My Breville is my new friend. It has a downlight so I can see what's going on in the shadowy corners of the mixing bowl, the bowl itself is glass so I can see all the ingredients have combined evenly, and it has a nifty timer, so I know exactly how long I've been creaming my butter. All these add-ons are luxurious for a die-hard baker.

Hand-held mixer

If you can't invest in a stand mixer, just use an electric hand-held mixer instead. Confession: when I first started my business that's all I had. I was churning out cupcake orders like a maniac, often with a mixer turned to full throttle in each hand. I'd burn out so many of them, but they were all I could use until the business got on its feet. In short, hand-held mixers can do the trick but it'll just take longer, and you'll need to be more diligent in ensuring your batters and doughs reach the right texture.

Blender or food processor

Whether it's a hand-held blender, food processor or a high-speed blender like a NutriBullet, you'll need something to blur your flavours together.

Juicer

When experimenting with vegetable-based recipes I always lean on my juicer (not literally). It is a vital friend for creating the liquid components that get used in caramels, cake soaks and syrups. I like juicers with an extra-wide chute for cramming whole beetroots into.

Steamer

Steaming vegetables and fruits helps to retain the colour and flavour of the produce better than boiling and tends to be quicker than roasting. I like to use the simple bamboo steamers that are widely available in Asian supermarkets.

Saucepan

You'll need at least one deep, heavy-based saucepan to make curds, custards and other fillings.

Oven thermometer

This is a cheap-as-chips addition to your kitchen that will keep you on track for cake heroics. If you love to cook, chances are your oven well worn; even though you think you have the right temperature, often the door seals aren't tight enough, or the flames aren't as strong as they should be. Pop a thermometer in the oven and you'll be 100 per cent assured that you're baking at the right setting and getting the best results.

Sugar thermometer

While you're in the thermometer aisle, pick up one of these guys – they're a must-have for hitting the mark making caramels and syrups, crystallising flowers and candying vegetables. I like the old-school glass thermometers that cost next to nothing; they seem to be more reliable than the electronic ones.

Electronic scales

Retro scales look great on a shelf, but they are not your friend in cake land. Electronic scales are the most accurate. No ifs or buts.

Measuring equipment

A cup is *not* your favourite coffee mug. A tablespoon is *not* your average cutlery tablespoon. Measuring cups and spoons *will* help you tell the difference.

Salad spinner

A simple gadget to dry washed herbs and flowers.

Whisk

Hand whisking still has value. It's ideal for delivering a light touch on meringues, creams and custards and for folding together dry ingredients.

Spatulas

For years, I never really understood the majesty of a spatula, always seeing them as an unnecessary invention. I was wrong. These rubber babes are the only way to scrape your bowls to perfection. While this may sound like a small thing, without it you might not combine your ingredients correctly and that's where fallen cakes or peaked, cracked cakes happen. Love your spatulas. I have thin, pliable ones with long handles to get into the awkward spots. I also rely on small metal spatulas to even out poured batters and ice cakes to a smooth finish.

Knives

A paring knife is very helpful for peeling and prepping your vegetables and trimming your herbs and flowers. Invest in a longer knife and use it to razor off the tops of cakes and cleanly shape brownies and slices. Don't use a serrated one for this – it will drag along the cooked cake layers and cause a mess. Keep your knives in good condition with a knife sharpener.

Fine-mesh sieve

I like to use a fine-mesh sieve for making small-batch purées – it's nice to do this by hand rather than getting the food processor out every time you need to make a paste.

Microplane

This little tool will finely shave citrus zest and spices, or mince ginger to an easily incorporated consistency.

Mandoline

For paper-thin vegetable slices, use a mandoline. It will give an elegant look to your decorations and creates the perfect thickness for crunchy dehydrated or oven-roasted root vegetables.

Aluminium cake tins, muffin tins and trays

Aluminium gives you a faster, more even bake than regular coated tins and trays. I prefer them to silicone moulds too, which I don't entirely trust to not get my bake stuck in the edges. For the most stress-free bake, lined aluminium cake tins, muffin tins and trays are your safest bet.

Wire rack

An essential for cooling your cakes, cookies and brownies without giving them soggy bottoms.

Cake decorating turntable

Just like a potter's wheel, this item helps you spin and smooth. It makes silky icing appear effortless, and is essential for giving your cakes that clean iced finish. The spinning motion is a very hypnotic end to an afternoon of baking.

Bench scraper and dustpan

Avoid using a wet cloth to scrape away sticky dough, flour or icing sugar. You will only make things worse. Allocate a dustpan and brush for worktop surfaces and buy a metal bench scraper to clean up in a jiffy.

Airtight containers

Essential for storing your baked goods once you've made them. Plus, even if you're an occasional baker, you'll want to ensure all your ingredients remain fresh and ready to whip out when your next baking mood strikes. Don't use elastic bands or pegs to seal your dry goods. Keep them in a snug bubble in containers. Label them. Feel organised.

Cake walk

Now you have your basic toolkit in place, let's bake. My heart belongs to cakes, so I'm going to take you through my methods for doing all things cake-related. I'm completely self-taught, so my knowledge is practical and my tips are tried and tested over ten years of baking mishaps and successes. I've done the failing for you, so you don't have to.

Pick your recipe
Read it all the way through. Baking meltdowns happen when you think you're flying through the method only to realise you've forgotten a crucial step. Read the steps carefully and jot down your own notes alongside it if you have to. Some of my most-loved cookbooks have my scribbles and question marks against recipes. It makes the experience even more meaningful when you return to the recipe, and your notes take you back to your first attempt (which was hopefully successful).

Keep it clean
Yawn. Bear with me though! You've set aside time to bake an A-class indulgence, you've prepped all the fresh ingredients and you've promised yourself to follow the recipe through this time – now, please, don't forget to clean as you go. There's nothing worse than feeling on top of the world for getting a cake in the oven only to step back and survey the kitchen insanity you've created, so chip off the cleaning in little chunks. Wear an apron, wash dishes as you go and put ingredients away after you use them. If you learn how to whisk and fold in a calm environment it'll make you want to bake more and more. And the more you bake, the better the baker you become.

Use room-temperature eggs, milk and butter
Cold ingredients can seize up batters and create an uneven bake. Get these ingredients to room temperature before you begin anything else.

Preheat your oven
Essential, obviously.

Start creaming your butter
Most baking recipes start with creaming the butter together with the sugar and flavourings, a step that helps to create air bubbles and is a sure bet for giving your bakes a light texture. Because it takes at least 6–10 minutes to get the mixture nice and fluffy I like to get on with this creaming before any other prepping, including lining the tins and measuring out the other ingredients.

Eyes on the beater
All the good stuff always gets caught in the beater. After each session of mixing, pick off the flavourful ingredients from the beaters and return them to the main batter. While you're there, scrape down the sides of the bowl for anything the beaters haven't picked up.

Line your cake tin
Don't even think about skipping this; greasing alone just doesn't cut it. I like to coat my tins with a mild-flavoured spray-on oil and then line them with baking paper. Line the sides of your tin first, then cut out the paper base slightly larger than the tin diameter. That way, when you push the base into the tin it helps hold down the paper on the sides and seals off any sneaky gaps. There's now no chance of your cake sticking to the tin and turning into a lumpy mess when you flip it out.

Get your rising agents in early
Try to drop your baking powder and bicarbonate of soda into your batter right after the stage in the recipe where you add the eggs. This gives your cake a head start for absorbing the rising agents and the longer those babies are mingling in your batter, the more chance you have of an even rise.

Measure and whisk your dry ingredients
I don't sift any flours because I can't tell the difference between a sifted and unsifted cake. When I read Christina Tosi from Momofuku Milk Bar felt the same way, my mind was set. I do, however, lightly whisk my flour together with my other dry ingredients, like cocoa, to give them a head start in the mixing bowl.

Fill your tin three-quarters high

This varies depending on how high your tins are, and most professional bakers recommend filling tins halfway, but I lean on the side of generous. It's a real drag when you spend time creating a beautiful cake but don't fill the tins enough, so your finished cake looks flat and mean.

Don't splash the sides

Pour your batter into the tin slowly and carefully, and smooth it over with a spatula so it's level. Remove any licks of batter from the sides because they'll burn and keep your cake from rising.

Weigh your tins

If you're making a layer cake, give yourself a hand and measure each tin to ensure they have the same amount of batter in them. This will mean each layer will bake to similar heights. This trick is essential for layer cakes with scraped-back icing, where you can't hide any errors.

Get even

Place your cake tin in the centre of the oven for the best airflow, bake for the allocated time and try not to open the oven door to sneak a peek, as opening the door can release warm air and ruin delicate cakes.

Test your cake by nudging the centre

If he bounces back, he's ready for you. Now, insert a thin skewer into the centre of the cake and check that it comes out clean with a few moist crumbs. You don't want the crumbs to be wet because that means the centre is gooey, and you don't want the crumbs to be dry as that means the cake is overcooked.

Cool then flip

Once the cake is out of the oven, leave it to cool for five minutes. Gently run a metal spatula or butter knife around the rim of the tin to unhinge any crusty bits, then take a clean tea towel and place it over the top of the warm cake. Place your palm gently over the tea towel, channel your inner Harlem Globetrotter and spread your fingers out really wide, then flip that tin with confidence and give it a little wiggle to set the cake free. Pop the cake onto a wire rack to cool down completely.

Trim

With a very sharp knife, pierce the side of your cooled cake at the point that has the lowest height. Insert the knife smoothly and rotate the cake with your other hand to make an even top. Trimmed cake layers give you a flat surface to fill and ice, and make each cut cake slice look tidy and pretty.

Ice

I like to go easy on icing. The cake is the hero and the topping is a sidekick. Italian meringue buttercream and caramel ganaches are my VIP toppings, but a good old icing sugar buttercream is always easy to flavour with new twists. To avoid an explosion of icing sugar when you beat the ingredients together, mix them by hand first before turning the mixer on. Cover the edge of the bowl with a tea towel to avoid any extra spills. I like to beat the icing slow and low at first then crank it to high speed for around six minutes, or until it's super fluffy.

Freezing is A-OK

Once your cake is cooled, give it a little chill time in the freezer before icing. Your icing will go on smooth and clean, and you'll be able to skip the old-fashioned crumb coating method, which can be time-consuming and messy as hell. (For the uninitiated, crumb coating is when you seal the edges of the fresh, cooled cake with a super thin layer of icing before a second coating is applied, and then the actual icing layer.)

Make it pretty

I like to keep things free-form and organic, so all my decorations are either edible or rambling garden florals. For me, robust flavours need pared-back icing and a bounty of earthy decorations. Scraped-back edges and straight-backed cakes are my trademark looks.

Share

Okay, you can totally burrow away on your own and eat your cake in solitude but, for me, the biggest pleasure is to serve up a huge slice of cake to one of your people. Cakes have the incredible capacity to bring excitement to any dinner table, so plonk your cake down in the middle and enjoy the reaction it brings.

Store in an airtight container

This is ideal for cakes without any icing. The container will keep your cake moist and perfect for nibbling on whenever a munchie moment hits. For iced cakes, store them in the fridge until the icing sets, then cover them with plastic wrap to avoid any fridge smells penetrating. I keep my cakes for no more than four days after baking.

Baking should be a fun, honest experience. Use quality ingredients and make every bite count.

PS *(tips and troubleshooting)*

Naturally, I love creating all kinds of baked goods, not just cakes. Over the years I've discovered a bevy of tidbits and lessons to help with troubleshooting in the kitchen.

Cookies will spread

It will make you sad, but if your cookie dreams have been shattered because they've unravelled into a puddle of dough, there is still hope. While the cookies are still warm from the oven, use a cookie cutter to punch out shapes in the soft dough. Allow them to cool and set. No one will ever know you cheated.

DIY self-raising flour

Bought the wrong flour? Grab 150 g (5½ oz/1 cup) of plain (all-purpose) flour and whisk it together with 2 teaspoons of baking powder and use it as a substitute for the equivalent quantity of self-raising flour.

DIY buttermilk

For a tangy home-made buttermilk, whisk a tablespoon of freshly squeezed lemon juice (or white vinegar) into every 250 ml (8½ fl oz/1 cup) of full-cream milk.

Pass the salt

I like to use kosher salt or fine sea salt flakes for my baking. They're not as sharp as table salt and absorb more subtly into the batter.

Use your extras

If 24 cookies seems like too much for one household (never), then most cookie recipes can be rolled into logs and wrapped in plastic wrap for freezing. Cut off a round of frozen dough and bake them one by one as each hunger pang hits.

Bake your pies in glass dishes

It's a cool way to check that the underside of your pie is browned and cooked.

Fight funky odours

Keep a cup of bicarbonate of soda at the back of your fridge or freezer to absorb that refrigerated smell and prevent any odours from penetrating your baked darlings.

Measure it out

- This book uses 15 ml (½ fl oz) tablespoons; cooks with 20 ml (¾ fl oz) tablespoons should be scant with their tablespoon measurements.

- Metric cup measurements are used, i.e. 250 ml (8½ fl oz) for 1 cup; in the US a cup is 237 ml (8 fl oz), so American cooks should be generous with their cup measurements; in the UK, a cup is 284 ml (9½ fl oz), so British cooks should be scant with their cup measurements.

- All eggs used in the recipes are 70 g (2½ oz), organic and room temperature unless otherwise specified. Milk should be full fat unless otherwise specified.

- Ovens should be preheated to the temperatures specified. If using a fan-forced oven, follow the manufacturer's instructions for adjusting the time and temperature.

Cakes

Golden saffron pumpkin

The warm, honey-like notes of saffron lend the pumpkin-flecked batter of this cake an addictive quality. Nasturtium butter helps form the cake's base – adding to its sunset looks and grassy, garden vibe – while the egg yolks deepen the colour and give it a lovely crumbly texture.

SERVES 8–10

150 g (5½ oz/1 cup)
  butternut pumpkin
  (squash), cut into 1 cm
  (½ in) cubes

5 g (¼ oz/¼ cup)
  nasturtium, marigold or
  calendula petals

230 g (8 oz/1 cup) caster
  (superfine) sugar

170 g (6 oz) unsalted
  butter

4 teaspoons saffron
  threads

6 egg yolks

1 egg

300 g (10½ oz/2 cups) plain
  (all-purpose) flour

½ teaspoon baking powder

½ teaspoon bicarbonate of
  soda (baking soda)

icing sugar, to serve

whipped cream, to serve

Add the pumpkin to a steamer set over a saucepan of lightly simmering water and cook until tender. Remove from the heat and set aside to cool, then mash 80 g (2¾ oz/½ cup) of the pumpkin in a bowl until smooth.

Preheat the oven to 175°C (345°F). Lightly grease and line a 20 cm (8 in) round cake tin with baking paper.

In a bowl, rub the flower petals into the sugar using your fingertips. Don't be delicate here; the more you rub, the more the petals will infuse their flavour into the sugar.

In the bowl of an electric mixer, beat the sugar and petal mixture together with the butter and saffron threads for 6 minutes on high speed until creamy and voluminous. Continue to beat on low speed, adding the egg yolks one by one followed by the whole egg, then adding the mashed pumpkin, flour, baking powder and bicarbonate of soda. Mix together until combined.

Pour the batter into the prepared tin, then gently push 35 g (1¼ oz/ ¼ cup) of the cooked pumpkin pieces into the batter so they're evenly distributed. Bake for 45 minutes, or until a skewer inserted into the centre comes out clean.

Remove the cake from the oven and leave to cool slightly in the tin for 5 minutes, then carefully turn out onto a wire rack and leave to cool completely. Sprinkle with icing sugar and serve with freshly whipped cream.

—

SAVE THOSE EGGSHELLS
This recipe will give you a good batch of shells to reuse in your garden. Crushed coarsely they make an excellent slug and snail repellent and add calcium to your soil, which can be a great boost to your tomato, beetroot and capsicum plants.

—

SEEDY START
For a sprawling blaze of colour, soak nasturtium seeds in water to encourage germination. The perfect home for nasturtiums is at the base of citrus trees with access to morning sun.

Porcini caramel and chestnut

SERVES 10–12

200 g (7 oz) unsalted butter

440 g (15½ oz/2 cups) sugar

1 teaspoon vanilla extract

4 eggs

250 g (9 oz/1 cup) sour cream

250 ml (8½ fl oz/1 cup) Mushroom cream (see below)

300 g (10½ oz/2 cups) plain (all-purpose) flour

90 g (3 oz/1 cup) chestnut flour

2 teaspoons baking powder

1 teaspoon bicarbonate of soda (baking soda)

1 teaspoon salt

figs, to serve

MUSHROOM CREAM

10 g (¼ oz) dried porcini mushrooms

625 ml (21 fl oz/2½ cups) thick (double/heavy) cream

PORCINI CARAMEL

110 g (4 oz/½ cup) sugar

2 tablespoons light corn syrup

60 ml (2 fl oz/¼ cup) water

185 ml (6 fl oz/¾ cup) Mushroom cream (see above)

To make the mushroom cream, add the porcini mushrooms and cream to a saucepan and bring to a gentle, frothy boil. Reduce the heat to low and simmer for 10 minutes, until slightly reduced and deeply fragrant. Strain into a container, pressing down gently on the porcini with a fork to extract the last of the liquid. Discard the porcini.

For the porcini caramel, carefully stir the sugar, corn syrup and water together in a small, high-sided saucepan set over a medium–high heat. Using a sugar thermometer to check, bring the mixture to a temperature of 180°C (350°F), then remove from the heat and leave to rest for 1 minute. Using a metal whisk, slowly stir 185 ml (6 fl oz/¾ cup) of the mushroom cream into the hot syrup mixture (the remainder will be used in the cake so don't throw it away or drink it) for 2–3 minutes until the caramel settles. Set aside.

Preheat the oven to 180°C (350°F). Lightly grease and line a 22 cm (9 in) square cake tin with baking paper.

Beat the butter, sugar and vanilla together in a large bowl for 10 minutes until creamy. Add the eggs one at a time, followed by the sour cream and 250 ml (8½ fl oz/1 cup) of the mushroom cream. Fold in the flours and the other dry ingredients and mix together gently to combine.

Spoon the batter into the prepared tin and bake for 1 hour, or until a skewer inserted into the centre comes out clean.

Remove the cake from the oven and leave to cool slightly in the tin for 5 minutes, then carefully turn out onto a wire rack. While still warm, smother the cake in the porcini caramel and leave to set before serving.

—

MUSHROOMS LOVE COFFEE

Oyster mushrooms are among the easiest variety to grow at home. This isn't something I've tried myself, but one technique is to nestle mushroom spawn (easily sourced online) into a bag of used coffee grounds. Sealed and placed in a warm pocket of your home (the internet suggests under your bed!) you'll have the buds of mushy friends in around three weeks. You try it first.

Velvety and rustic, this is an autumnal cake filled with foraged ingredients. With its creamy, butterscotch vibe complete with a whisper of mushroom, the porcini caramel is one of my favourite surprises, while the chestnut flour gives the cake a nutty, fudgy texture. The cake's flavours seem to deepen when eaten a day later – try topping it with juicy figs and a spray of field flowers.

Parsnip, pear and cinnamon

Prepare this on a rainy Sunday when you're time-poor but craving a sophisticated, wholesome treat. Once baked, slice up a hefty wedge and spread it with creamy butter or pot-set yoghurt.

MAKES 1 LOAF

70 g (2½ oz/½ cup) pear, grated

125 ml (4 fl oz/½ cup) hazelnut oil

95 g (3¼ oz/½ cup) soft brown sugar

2 teaspoons ground cinnamon

2 teaspoons vanilla extract

2 eggs

225 g (8 oz/1½ cups) plain (all-purpose) flour

½ teaspoon baking powder

½ teaspoon bicarbonate of soda (baking soda)

½ teaspoon salt

130 g (4½ oz/1 cup) grated parsnip

60 g (2 oz/½ cup) hazelnuts, roughly chopped

Preheat the oven to 175°C (345°F). Lightly grease and line a 450 g (1 lb) loaf (bar) tin with baking paper.

Squeeze the grated pear to remove any excess moisture. Set aside.

Whisk together the oil, brown sugar, cinnamon and vanilla in a bowl using a hand-held mixer, or a stand mixer fitted with the whisk attachment, to combine. Beat in the eggs one by one, then stir in the flour, baking powder, bicarbonate of soda and salt and mix together well to form a batter. Gently fold in the grated parsnip, pear and chopped hazelnuts to incorporate evenly.

Pour the batter into the prepared tin and bake for 40 minutes, or until a skewer inserted into the centre comes out clean. Leave to cool slightly in the tin for 5 minutes, then turn out onto a wire rack and leave to cool completely.

—

HIBERNATE FOR TASTE

Parsnips thrive underground in winter. After two weeks of cold weather the chill converts the starch in the roots to sugars, which helps them develop their distinctive sweet, nutty flavour. Leave your parsnips in the ground for a few frosty months, snug under a blanket of mulch, and pull out your rewards in spring.

Coffee, banana and zucchini

A coffee and a banana – two breakfast staples for a fast-paced life. Here I've rolled these ingredients into a loaf, partnered them with zucchini and finished it off with a naughty butterscotch drizzle. For a gluten-free version, keep it in the family and use green banana flour – just reduce the flour measurement to 185 g (6½ oz/1¼ cups).

MAKES 1 LOAF

55 g (2 oz/¼ cup) raw (demerara) sugar

45 g (1½ oz/¼ cup) soft brown sugar

1 egg

80 ml (2½ fl oz/⅓ cup) grapeseed oil

15 g (½ oz/¼ cup) good-quality instant coffee

1 teaspoon vanilla extract

225 g (8 oz/1½ cups) wholemeal (whole-wheat) flour

1 teaspoon baking powder

½ teaspoon bicarbonate of soda (baking soda)

½ teaspoon salt

225 g (8 oz/1 cup) mashed very ripe bananas

135 g (5 oz/1 cup) grated zucchini (courgette)

BUTTERSCOTCH DRIZZLE

400 g (14 oz) soft brown sugar

100 g (3½ oz) unsalted butter

500 ml (17 fl oz/2 cups) thick (double/heavy) cream

Preheat the oven to 175°C (345°F). Lightly grease and line a 450 g (1 lb) loaf (bar) tin with baking paper.

Mix the sugars, egg, oil, coffee and vanilla together in a bowl until well combined. Sift over the flour, baking powder, bicarbonate of soda and salt and fold into the mixture, then add the banana and zucchini and fold together to combine.

Pour the batter into the prepared tin and bake for 1 hour, or until a skewer inserted into the centre comes out clean. Remove from the oven and leave to cool slightly in the tin for 5 minutes, then carefully turn out onto a wire rack and leave to cool completely.

For the butterscotch drizzle, add the ingredients to a heavy-based saucepan set over a medium-high heat and stir to combine. Bring to a simmer, then remove from the heat and drizzle over the cooled cake.

—

HANDS OFF

Zucchini are a great beginner's crop because they thrive on being left alone; once planted, you can literally sit back and let them run wild. Be watchful though, as you'll be surprised how quickly they can grow. Although giant zucchini are fun to show off with, try to pick them when they're young and tender for optimum moisture and flavour.

Chamomile and white chocolate

Soft and gentle chamomile runs through this buttery tea cake, spiked with the sweet sap of maple trees and the milkiness of white chocolate. Serve warm, to hit maximum comfort levels.

SERVES 10–12

5 g (¼ oz/¼ cup) chamomile petals

1 vanilla bean, split lengthways and seeds scraped

110 g (4 oz/½ cup) raw (demerara) sugar

2 eggs

140 ml (4½ fl oz) maple syrup, plus extra for serving

280 g (10 oz) unsalted butter, melted

170 g (6 oz) Greek-style yoghurt

250 g (9 oz/1⅔ cups) plain (all-purpose) flour

2 teaspoons baking powder

½ teaspoon salt

150 g (5½ oz) white chocolate chips

Preheat the oven to 175°C (345°F). Lightly grease and line a 22 cm (9 in) round cake tin with baking paper.

In a food processor, blitz together the chamomile petals, vanilla seeds and sugar to form a fine powder.

Beat the eggs together in a large bowl using a hand-held mixer, or a stand mixer fitted with the whisk attachment, until frothy. Add the maple syrup, melted butter, yoghurt and sugar mixture and beat again to combine. Fold in the flour, baking powder, salt and chocolate chips.

Pour the batter into the prepared tin and bake for 45 minutes, or until a skewer inserted into the centre comes out clean.

Remove from the oven, turn out onto a wire rack and leave to cool slightly. Serve warm with a drizzle of maple syrup.

—

BRING THE CALM INSIDE

Chamomile can be grown indoors facing a window that gets a few hours of sun each day. Planted from seed and cared for in moist soil, it will produce a plentiful mop of flowers in around 2–3 months, and provide some indoor greenery that makes a nice change from your everyday fern.

Tea pea

Matcha green tea has a bitter edge that balances beautifully with grassy garden peas. Add to them a subtle splash of tangy buttermilk and a little menthol-fresh peppermint, and the result is this creamy, robust little number. This cake is very easy to make and contains no butter – so you can get away with generous servings of the garden pea cream.

SERVES 10–12

15 g (½ oz/¾ cup) peppermint leaves, finely chopped

185 ml (6 fl oz/¾ cup) boiling water

400 g (14 oz/1¾ cups) caster (superfine) sugar

375 g (13 oz/2½ cups) plain (all-purpose) flour

3 tablespoons matcha green tea powder

1½ teaspoons bicarbonate of soda (baking soda)

1½ teaspoons baking powder

1½ teaspoons pink Himalayan salt

2 eggs

250 ml (8½ fl oz/1 cup) buttermilk

125 ml (4 fl oz/½ cup) grapeseed oil

1 vanilla bean, split lengthways and seeds scraped

1 teaspoon almond extract

pea tendrils and flowers, to decorate

GARDEN PEA CREAM

465 g (1 lb/3 cups) garden peas

750 ml (25½ fl oz/3 cups) whipping cream

3–4 tablespoons icing (confectioners') sugar

Preheat the oven to 175°C (345°F). Lightly grease and line a 22 cm (9 in) ring (bundt) tin with baking paper.

Add the peppermint leaves to a bowl, cover with the boiling water and set aside to steep for 5 minutes.

Meanwhile, in a separate bowl, mix together the sugar, flour, green tea powder, bicarbonate of soda, baking powder and salt.

In another bowl, lightly whisk the eggs together with the buttermilk and oil to combine, then whisk in the vanilla seeds and almond extract. Slowly fold the mixed dry ingredients into the egg mixture.

Strain the peppermint leaf water, discarding the leaves, and fold the water into the cake batter. Pour the batter into the prepared tin and bake for 30 minutes, or until a skewer inserted into the centre comes out clean. Remove from the oven and leave to cool slightly in the tin for 5 minutes, then carefully turn out onto a wire rack and leave to cool completely.

While the cake is cooling, make the garden pea cream. Add the peas to a blender and pulse briefly to a smooth, fine purée. In a bowl, whisk the cream to medium peaks, then fold in the pea purée. Add the icing sugar to taste.

Top with generous dollops of the pea cream and decorate with pea tendrils and flowers.

—

SMALL SPACES

While frozen peas are super convenient, they'll never beat a naked pea squeezed straight from a pod. Peas are perfect for tiny patches because they grow upwards, not outwards. Pot your seedlings in a sunny spot on your balcony or in your courtyard and, once sprouted, guide the sprawl of tendrils through trellises, nets, ladders or an inventive canopy of string. Most pea varieties will grow up to 2 m (6 ft 7 in) tall, so think ahead.

Rhubarb and pumpernickel

All the best sour ingredients meet up in this bittersweet cake. Tart rye joins forces with liqueur-spiked rhubarb, a chocolate herb ganache and a garnish of crispy rye croutons. A satisfying dessert for when the nights get colder.

SERVES 10–12

- 125 g (4½ oz/1 cup) Dutch (unsweetened) cocoa powder
- 250 ml (8½ fl oz/1 cup) boiling water
- 1 pumpernickel bread slice, torn into rough crumbs
- 3 tablespoons orange-flavoured liqueur (such as Cointreau)
- 225 g (8 oz) unsalted butter
- 185 g (6½ oz/1 cup) soft brown sugar
- 345 g (12 oz/1½ cups) caster (superfine) sugar
- 4 teaspoons molasses
- 4 eggs
- 1 teaspoon baking powder
- 2 teaspoons bicarbonate of soda (baking soda)
- 1 teaspoon salt
- 300 g (10½ oz/2 cups) plain (all-purpose) flour
- 100 g (3½ oz/1 cup) rye flour
- 250 g (9 oz/1 cup) sour cream
- 450 g (1 lb) rhubarb, cut into 2 cm (¾ in) pieces
- rosemary blossoms, to decorate

Preheat the oven to 175°C (345°F). Lightly grease and line individual mini bundt tins, a 12-hole standard muffin tin or a 22 cm (9 in) round cake tin with baking paper.

For the herb ganache, add the rosemary stalks and cream to a saucepan, bring to a simmer and leave to cook over a low heat for 5 minutes. Remove from the heat and set aside to cool and infuse.

For the rye croutons, cut the toasted rye bread slices into 5 mm (¼ in) squares. Melt the butter in a frying pan set over a medium–high heat, add the sugar and the bread squares and cook until caramelised and lightly crisp. Remove from the pan and set aside.

Stir the cocoa powder and boiling water together in a bowl to make a thick paste.

Add the pumpernickel breadcrumbs to a separate bowl, pour over the liqueur and set aside to soak while you prepare the rest of the cake.

Beat the butter, sugars and molasses together in the bowl of an electric mixer for 10 minutes, or until fluffy. Continuing to beat on a low speed, add the eggs one at a time, followed by the baking powder, bicarbonate of soda, salt and half of the flours. Add the sour cream, then the remainder of the dry ingredients. Pour over the chocolate paste and mix until evenly combined, then gently mix in the soaked pumpernickel and rhubarb.

Pour the batter into the prepared tin and bake for 25 minutes if using bundt or muffin tins, or 45 minutes if using a round cake tin, until a skewer inserted into the centre comes out clean. Leave to cool on a wire rack.

While the cakes are cooling, finish the ganache. Remove the rosemary stalks from the cream and add the dark chocolate, then transfer the mixture to a heatproof bowl set over a saucepan of lightly simmering water. Heat gently, stirring, until the chocolate has melted completely and the mixture is glossy.

Spread the ganache over the cooled cakes and decorate with the crispy rye croutons and a few rosemary blossoms.

HERB GANACHE

2 rosemary stalks

300 ml (10 fl oz) thick
   (double/heavy) cream

250 g (9 oz) good-quality
   dark chocolate (approx.
   60% cocoa solids), broken
   into chunks

RYE CROUTONS

2 dark rye bread slices,
   toasted and crusts
   removed

30 g (1 oz) unsalted butter

1½ tablespoons soft brown
   sugar

—
LONG-TIME COMPANION

Well-loved rhubarb can be productive for 10 years or more and has
a large root system, so plant it somewhere it can dig deep and nest.
For a faster yield, ask your nursery for rhubarb crowns or budded
pieces and start from there rather than growing from seed.

Burnt orange and smoked lavender

These no-fuss almond tea cakes, packed with bitter, chewy orange pieces and served with a smoky side of cream, are made for sharing. Be warned, you'll want at least two per person.

MAKES 12

1 orange, skin on and cut into 5 mm (¼ in) cubes

250 g (9 oz) unsalted butter

230 g (8 oz/1 cup) caster (superfine) sugar

a few drops of orange-blossom water

3 eggs

125 ml (4 fl oz/½ cup) milk

225 g (8 oz/1½ cups) plain (all-purpose) flour

55 g (2 oz/½ cup) ground almonds

2 teaspoons baking powder

½ teaspoon salt

SMOKED LAVENDER CREAM

500 ml (17 fl oz/2 cups) thick (double/heavy) cream

3 tablespoons dried lavender

Preheat the oven to 175°C (345°F). Line a 12-hole standard muffin tin with paper cases.

Add the orange pieces to a frying pan set over a high heat and cook for 10 minutes, stirring, until fragrant and charred. Remove from the heat and set aside.

Cream the butter, sugar and orange-blossom water together in a bowl using a hand-held mixer, or a stand mixer fitted with the paddle attachment, until light and fluffy. Add the eggs one at a time followed by the milk, then fold in the flour, ground almonds, baking powder and salt to form a batter.

Stir in the burnt orange pieces to distribute evenly, then divide the batter among the paper cases. Bake for 1 hour, or until a skewer inserted into the centre of a tea cake comes out clean. Remove from the oven and leave to cool slightly in the tin for 5 minutes, then transfer to a wire rack and leave to cool completely.

While the tea cakes are cooling, make the smoked lavender cream. Spoon the cream into a large bowl and cover with plastic wrap. Add the dried lavender to the burn chamber of a smoking gun and smoke the cream according to the manufacturer's instructions, being sure to only do this for a few seconds so as not to overdo the lavender fragrance.

Top the teacakes with a generous dollop of the smoked lavender cream before serving.

—

MOOD BOOSTER

For most of us, a waft of lavender conjures up feelings of relaxation. It's recently been discovered that this edible flower has similar calmative effects on bees too. Plant up some blue, purple or pink varieties in your yard to attract (and de-stress) these very helpful buzzers.

Nectarine and rosemary

Nothing flashy here, just classic friands packed with a combination of tart and earthy flavours. I love how the rosemary balances out the fruitiness of the stone fruit with a shrubby, herbal seasoning.

MAKES 12

4 nectarines, quartered and thinly sliced

95 g (3¼ oz/½ cup) soft brown sugar

300 g (10½ oz) unsalted butter, softened

3 tablespoons very finely sliced rosemary

10 egg whites

250 g (9 oz/2 cups) icing (confectioners') sugar

200 g (7 oz/2 cups) ground almonds

75 g (2¾ oz/½ cup) plain (all-purpose) flour

Preheat the oven to 180°C (350°F).

Sprinkle the nectarine pieces with the soft brown sugar and place under a hot grill for a few minutes until lightly caramelised. Set aside to cool.

Beat the butter and rosemary together in a bowl using a hand-held mixer, or a stand mixer fitted with the paddle attachment, for 6–8 minutes, or until the butter mixture is fragrant. Melt the rosemary butter in a saucepan over a low heat and set aside.

Whisk the egg whites together in a large bowl or a stand mixer to form soft peaks. Add the icing sugar, ground almonds, melted butter mixture and flour and whisk to form a batter.

Divide the batter evenly among 12 friand moulds and top each with a few nectarine slices. Bake for 45 minutes, or until a skewer inserted into the centre of a friand comes out clean. Leave to cool in the tin on a wire rack until ready to serve.

—

TOUGH LOVE

Once your rosemary has flowered and you've used the blossoms in your baking, cut the shrub right back to continue growth. Be harsh with your pruning. A small, bald rosemary bush will yield far better leaves than one that's left to grow wild and woody.

Chocolate, potato and stout

SERVES 8–10

150 g (5½ oz) potato, peeled and cut into cubes

150 g (5½ oz) good-quality dark chocolate (approx. 60% cocoa solids), broken into chunks

500 g (1 lb 2 oz) unsalted butter

400 g (14 oz) soft brown sugar

8 eggs

300 g (10½ oz/2 cups) plain (all-purpose) flour

50 g (1¾ oz) Dutch (unsweetened) cocoa powder

2 teaspoons baking powder

1 teaspoon bicarbonate of soda (baking soda)

300 ml (10 fl oz) stout beer

MERINGUE ICING

120 ml (4 fl oz/½ cup) water

550 g (19 oz/2½ cups) sugar

10 egg whites, at room temperature

Add the potato to a saucepan of boiling water and cook until tender. Drain, return to the pan and mash until smooth, then set aside to cool.

Preheat the oven to 175°C (345°F). Lightly grease and line three 15 cm (6 in) round cake tins with baking paper.

Place the chocolate in a bowl set over a saucepan of lightly simmering water and melt gently, stirring, until completely smooth. Remove from the heat.

Beat the butter and sugar together in a large bowl until pale and fluffy. Add the melted chocolate and eggs and beat well, then stir in the mashed potato. Sift over the flour, cocoa, baking powder and bicarbonate of soda and gently mix together, pouring in the stout as you go to form a batter.

Divide the batter evenly among the prepared tins and bake for 30 minutes, or until a skewer inserted into the centre of each comes out clean. Remove the cakes from the oven and leave to cool slightly in the tins for 5 minutes, then carefully turn out onto a wire rack and leave to cool completely.

While the cakes are cooling, make the meringue. Add the water and 440 g (16 oz/2 cups) of the sugar to a saucepan, stir to dissolve and bring to the boil. Using a sugar thermometer to check, bring the mixture to a temperature of 180°C (350°F).

Meanwhile, whisk the egg whites together in a bowl using an electric mixer on high speed until stiff peaks form. Add the remaining sugar, reduce the mixer to medium speed and continue to whisk, slowly adding the hot sugar syrup, for 8 minutes or until the meringue is thick and glossy and the bowl is cool to the touch.

Place one of the cooled cakes on a serving plate or stand and spread with a quarter of the icing. Repeat with a second cake. Place the third cake on top and spoon the remaining icing over the top and sides, using the back of the spoon to make light indents in it to create peaks and swirls. To finish, use a blowtorch to lightly toast the meringue peaks.

—

SAVE YOUR GNARLY POTATOES

Old and ugly, these guys can be replanted to generate your very own potato crop. Making sure your potatoes have a few 'eyes' sprouting, simply cut them in half and leave them to dry overnight, before planting them in a well-composted soil trench about 20 cm (8 in) deep and 10 cm (4 in) apart. New shoots should appear in a few weeks.

Buttery mashed potato often ranks in people's top-five comfort foods. If (like me) your eyes are bigger than your belly, try saving two-thirds of a cup of leftover mash for this hearty cake. The pillowy mash lightens up the dense, malty flavours of the stout beer and dark chocolate, while the toasted meringue icing mimics the head of a well-poured Guinness. For an added lick of cocoa, look into getting your hands on a boutique chocolate stout.

Sweet potato and Czech poppy seed

During a trip to Prague I gorged myself on *makový závin*, a pastry loaded with bittersweet poppy seeds – a total danger zone for toothy smiles. This is a riff on that memory. The poppy seed filling swirls around a subtle, dense sweet potato cake studded with pecans. An excellent companion for a mug of strong black coffee.

SERVES 10–12

260 g (9 oz) sweet potato, peeled and cut into cubes

4 eggs

3 tablespoons vanilla extract

185 g (6½ oz/1 cup) soft brown sugar

160 ml (5½ fl oz) sunflower oil

375 g (13 oz/2⅔ cups) plain (all-purpose) flour

2 teaspoons bicarbonate of soda (baking soda)

2 teaspoons ground ginger

½ teaspoon salt

100 g (3½ oz/1 cup) pecans, chopped

CZECH POPPY SEED FILLING

225 g (8 oz/1½ cups) poppy seeds

zest of 1 orange

45 g (1½ oz) sultanas (golden raisins)

45 g (1½ oz/¼ cup) soft brown sugar

2 teaspoons honey

4 teaspoons unsalted butter, melted

25 g (1 oz/¼ cup) ground almonds

zest of 1 lemon

Add the sweet potato to a steamer set over a saucepan of lightly simmering water and cook until tender. Remove from the heat and set aside to cool, then blitz to a smooth purée using a food processor or hand-held blender.

Preheat the oven to 175°C (345°F). Lightly grease and line a 22 cm (9 in) ring (bundt) tin with baking paper.

To make the poppy seed filling, put the poppy seeds in a bowl, cover with boiling water and leave to soak for 5 minutes. Drain, then transfer to a food processor and blitz together with the orange zest and sultanas, then add the sugar, honey, melted butter, ground almonds and lemon zest and blitz again to combine.

Beat the eggs, vanilla, sugar and oil together in a bowl using a hand-held mixer, or a stand mixer fitted with the paddle attachment, for 2–3 minutes until smooth. Add the flour, bicarbonate of soda, ginger and salt one by one and continue to beat until thoroughly combined, then beat in the sweet potato purée and pecans until evenly distributed. Gently fold in the poppy seed mixture.

Spoon the batter into the prepared tin and bake for 35 minutes, or until a skewer inserted into the centre comes out clean. Remove from the oven and leave to cool slightly in the tin for 5 minutes, then carefully turn out onto a wire rack and leave to cool completely.

—

SUNSHINE VINE

Although sweet potatoes are commonly grown as a perennial ground cover, with eagle-eyed pruning and plenty of sunlight they'll be right at home in a sturdy vertical garden or hanging over a rooftop ledge.

Spiced parsnip and blossom

SERVES 10-12

1 teaspoon coriander seeds

½ teaspoon star anise

200 g (7 oz) soft brown sugar

100 g (3½ oz) raw (demerara) sugar

4 teaspoons blossom water (such as wild-willow water or orange-blossom water)

300 ml (10 fl oz) grapeseed oil

3 eggs

300 g (10½ oz/2 cups) plain (all-purpose) flour

1 teaspoon baking powder

1 teaspoon bicarbonate of soda (baking soda)

½ teaspoon sea salt flakes

330 g (11½ oz/4 cups) grated parsnip

2 teaspoons finely grated fresh ginger

4 teaspoons finely chopped coriander (cilantro) stalks

BLOSSOM ICING

600 g (1 lb 5 oz) icing (confectioners') sugar

2-3 drops of blossom water

100 g (3½ oz) unsalted butter, softened

250 g (9 oz) cream cheese, chilled

Preheat the oven to 175°C (345°F). Lightly grease and line a 22 cm (9 in) round cake tin with baking paper.

Blitz the coriander seeds and star anise in a food processor or spice grinder to form a powder. Set aside, separating ½ teaspoon for garnishing.

Beat the sugars, blossom water, oil and eggs together in a large bowl until frothy and well combined.

Mix the flour, baking powder, bicarbonate of soda and salt together in a separate bowl to combine. Fold the flour mixture into the egg mixture in two batches, then stir in the parsnip, ginger, coriander stalks and freshly ground spices (remembering to set aside ½ teaspoon of the spices for garnishing) and mix together well.

Pour the batter into the prepared tin and bake for 30-40 minutes, or until a skewer inserted into the centre comes out clean. Remove from the oven and leave to cool slightly in the tin for 5 minutes, then carefully turn out onto a wire rack and leave to cool completely.

While the cake is cooling, make the icing. Add the icing sugar, blossom water and butter to the bowl of a stand mixer and beat together on medium-slow speed until the mixture comes together. Add the cream cheese and beat on medium-high speed for at least 5 minutes, or until fluffy and smooth.

Place the cooled cake on a serving plate or stand and spread with the icing.

—

BRUTES TO GROW

Parsnips have a reputation for being a tricky vegetable to cultivate, because when planted from seed it will take around 100 days for anything to appear. To encourage healthy growth, water with a seaweed fertiliser twice a month and ... wait.

—

MULTIPLE BLOOMS

Citrus blossoms can bud several times per year so make the most of the flowering periods with a DIY blossom water. Wash the petals thoroughly and dice finely, then transfer them to a bowl and cover with distilled water and a dash of vodka. Refrigerate overnight. The next day, bring the mixture to a gentle boil in a saucepan over a medium-high heat, reduce to a simmer and cook gently for 30 minutes. Leave to cool, then strain and store in a sterilised jar.

The poor parsnip often gets lost in a tray of mixed roasted vegetables, but it's far more interesting than you might think. This moist cake celebrates its overlooked flavours and pairs them with the floral tones of blossom water. I like using wild-willow water, which is a lighter Persian alternative to rosewater, but you could also use orange-blossom water – either will add a fresh, sweet hum. If it's a special occasion, top your blossom icing with flowers (I like to use stock) and sprinkle with ground ginger.

Viola syrup

MAKES 12

250 g (9 oz) unsalted butter

230 g (8 oz/1 cup) caster (superfine) sugar

2 vanilla beans, split lengthways and seeds scraped

3 eggs

125 ml (4 fl oz/½ cups) milk

300 g (10½ oz/2 cups) plain (all-purpose) flour

2 teaspoons baking powder

½ teaspoon salt

500 g (1 lb 2 oz/2 cups) labneh

VIOLA SYRUP

3 tablespoons violas, plus extra to decorate

250 g (9 oz) sugar

500 ml (17 fl oz/2 cups) water

Preheat the oven to 175°C (345°F). Line a 12-hole standard muffin or friand tin with paper cases.

Cream the butter, sugar and vanilla seeds together in a bowl with a hand-held mixer, or in a stand mixer fitted with the paddle attachment, until light and fluffy. Gently beat in the eggs one at a time followed by the milk, flour, baking powder and salt to form a batter.

Pour the batter into the prepared tin and bake for around 45 minutes, or until a skewer inserted into the centre of one of the tea cakes comes out clean.

While the tea cakes are baking, make the viola syrup. Using your hands, rub the violas into the sugar in a bowl until the flowers are thoroughly mashed (you want maximum petal power in here, so don't be afraid to be rough). Add the viola sugar mixture and water to a saucepan on a low heat and stir to dissolve, then increase the heat to medium–low and simmer for 15 minutes, or until the mixture is thick and syrupy.

Remove the tea cakes from the oven and pour a tablespoon of the warm syrup over each while still hot. Leave to cool slightly in the tin for 5 minutes, then transfer to a wire rack and leave to cool completely.

To serve, spoon a generous dollop of labneh on top of each cake. Finish with a generous drizzle of the remaining syrup and decorate with the violas.

—

TOUGH AND TEENY

A colourful ground cover for vegetable patches, violas can tolerate cool shade from towering edible neighbours and shivery conditions from frosty mornings. Mightier than they appear, they even help banish pests like aphids and cabbage moth.

These little tea cakes are soaked in irresistible honey-lemon tones from the purple-tinged viola syrup. A dollop of sharp labneh – a strained yoghurt with the texture of goat's cheese – is a nice switch from regular cream, and creates the perfect vessel for the syrup to linger. Make your own labneh by hanging full-fat Greek-style yoghurt in muslin (cheesecloth) and squeezing out the liquid until it's a firm, creamy ball.

Simple geranium butter cake

A classic butter cake infused with scented geraniums every step of the way. Baking doesn't get much easier than this. Just be sure to start things off the day before to allow the flavour of the geranium leaves to really work its way into the sugar and butter. Sincere and nurturing, this is a recipe you'll soon learn by heart.

SERVES 10–12

10–12 scented geranium leaves

230 g (8 oz/1 cup) caster (superfine) sugar

250 g (9 oz) unsalted butter

3 eggs

1 vanilla bean, split lengthways and seeds scraped

125 ml (4 fl oz/½ cup) milk

300 g (10½ oz/2 cups) self-raising flour

Set aside eight geranium leaves. Rub and scrunch the remainder in your hands to release their scented oil. Place two of the rubbed leaves in a container with the sugar and seal with the lid, then wrap the butter in the remaining scrunched leaves. Leave both ingredients to stand at room temperature overnight.

When ready to bake, preheat the oven to 175°C (345°F) and line a 22 cm (9 in) round cake tin with baking paper.

Remove the geranium leaves from the butter and sugar and beat the two ingredients together in a bowl using a hand-held mixer, or a stand mixer with the paddle attachment, for 6 minutes until light and fluffy. Beat in the eggs, vanilla seeds and milk, then gently fold in the flour to form a batter (being careful not to overwork the mixture).

Arrange the whole, unscrunched geranium leaves over the base and sides of the prepared tin, pour over the batter and top with more geranium leaves. Bake for 1 hour, or until a skewer inserted into the centre comes out clean. Remove from the oven and leave to cool slightly in the tin for 5 minutes, then transfer to a wire rack and leave to cool completely.

Once the cake is cool, and before you eat it, carefully remove the leaves from the cake (this should leave you with pretty indentations on the top and sides).

—

NO EXCUSES

Scented geraniums are one of the easiest edibles to grow. There are just under 100 different scents to experiment with, including apple, strawberry, chocolate mint, ginger and nutmeg. Brilliant as an indoor or outdoor potted plant, they're an exciting addition to your kitchen-scape. Growing them is just as exciting because it's oh so easy. Plant from cuttings, water only when the soil dries out and keep them in direct sunlight (careful not to burn them).

Pumpkin bourbon crunch

Pumpkin's creamy tones and mousse-like texture are far too delicious to save for Halloween or Thanksgiving. I wanted to treat these guys to a new flavour twist, so I've given them some tender loving care with a healthy splash of bourbon, some crispy bacon pieces and crushed amaretti biscuits.

SERVES 8–10

4 cloves

600 g (1 lb 5 oz) soft brown sugar

6 eggs

½ teaspoon vanilla extract

60 ml (2 fl oz/¼ cup) bourbon

600 ml (20½ fl oz) grapeseed oil

1 teaspoon finely grated fresh ginger

375 g (13 oz/2½ cups) plain (all-purpose) flour

2 teaspoons baking powder

2 teaspoons bicarbonate of soda (baking soda)

1 teaspoon salt

500 g (1 lb 2 oz) grated butternut pumpkin (squash)

PUMPKIN ICING

170 g (6 oz) butternut pumpkin, cut into cubes

250 g (9 oz) cream cheese

80 g (2¾ oz) unsalted butter, at room temperature

850 g (1 lb 14 oz) icing (confectioners') sugar, plus extra if necessary

25 ml (¾ fl oz) bourbon

Preheat the oven to 175°C (345°F). Lightly grease and line two 20 cm (8 in) round cake tins with baking paper.

In a food processor or spice grinder, blitz the cloves to form a powder. Set aside.

Whisk the sugar, eggs, vanilla, bourbon, oil and ginger together in a mixing bowl. Fold in the ground cloves, flour, baking powder, bicarbonate of soda and salt and mix well, then add the grated pumpkin and mix together to form a batter.

Divide the batter evenly between the prepared tins and bake for 45 minutes, or until the sponges are golden brown and a skewer inserted into the centres comes out clean. Remove from the oven and leave the sponges to cool slightly in the tins for 5 minutes, then carefully turn out onto a wire rack and leave to cool completely.

Meanwhile, make the icing. Steam the pumpkin until tender, then transfer to a food processor and blend to a purée. Add the puréed pumpkin to the bowl of a stand mixer together with the remaining ingredients and beat together until light and fluffy, adding a little extra icing sugar if the icing is looking a little loose.

PUMPKIN CRUNCH

50 g (1¾ oz/½ cup) amaretti
  biscuits (cookies),
  crushed

100 g (3½ oz/¾ cup) pepitas
  (pumpkin seeds), toasted

300 g (10½ oz/1 cup) almond
  butter

40 g (1½ oz) bacon rashers
  (slices), diced and
  grilled until crispy

80 g (2¾ oz/⅔ cup) icing
  (confectioners') sugar

4 teaspoons unsalted
  butter, melted

For the pumpkin crunch, mix together all the ingredients in a bowl with your fingertips to form crunchy clusters.

Place one of the cooled cakes on a serving plate or stand, spread with half the icing and sprinkle over half the pumpkin crunch. Place the second cake on top, spread with the remaining icing and top with the rest of the crunch to finish.

—

SPACE TO THRIVE

Pumpkins really love to stretch out and explore, so sow your seeds at the edge of your vegetable patch so they don't suffocate your other edibles. For something different, encourage smaller pumpkin varieties to grow downwards from burly hanging pots.

Pimm's, cucumber and borage

I went through a big phase of making cocktail-themed cakes. During that time mojito, tequila sunrise and champagne bellini-inspired creations were my boozy remedy for summer wedding cake orders. Similarly, this pound cake packs a fruity alcoholic kick, though the cucumber and borage syrup lends it a bright, refreshing finish.

SERVES 10–12

1 cucumber

5 g (¼ oz/¼ cup) peppermint leaves

515 g (1 lb 2 oz/2¼ cups) caster (superfine) sugar

455 g (1 lb) unsalted butter

zest of 2 oranges

zest of 1 lemon

9 eggs

450 g (1 lb/3 cups) plain (all-purpose) flour

3 teaspoons baking powder

2 teaspoons salt

185 g (6½ oz/¾ cup) sour cream

150 g (5½ oz/1 cup) fresh strawberries, hulled and quartered

CUCUMBER BORAGE SYRUP

1 cucumber, cut into rough chunks

200 ml (7 fl oz) Pimm's

10 g (¼ oz/⅓ cup) fresh borage flowers

100 g (3½ oz) caster (superfine) sugar

3 tablespoons orange juice

Preheat the oven to 175°C (345°F). Lightly grease and line a 22 cm (9 in) round cake tin with baking paper.

Peel the cucumber, reserving the peel. Using your hands, rub the peppermint leaves and cucumber peel into the caster sugar in a bowl until well combined. Add the cucumber flesh to a food processor and blitz to a purée. Set aside.

Cream the butter, orange and lemon zests and sugar mixture together in a bowl using a hand-held mixer, or a stand mixer fitted with the paddle attachment, until fluffy. Mix in the eggs one at a time followed by half the flour, baking powder and salt. Stir in the sour cream and cucumber purée, then add the remaining dry ingredients and mix to form a batter.

Folding gently, drop the strawberry pieces into the batter in small handfuls until evenly distributed. Pour the batter into the prepared tin and bake for 1½ hours, or until a skewer inserted into the centre comes out clean.

While the cake is baking, make the syrup. Pass the cucumber pieces through a juicer. Transfer 100 ml (3½ fl oz) of the juice to a high-sided saucepan with all the remaining ingredients and cook over a medium heat, stirring, for about 6 minutes, or until the sugar has dissolved and the mixture is thick and syrupy.

Once cooked, remove the cake from the oven and transfer to a wire rack. Pour over the syrup evenly and leave to cool slightly, then remove from the tin and leave to cool completely.

PIMM'S ICING

600 g (1 lb 5 oz) icing
  (confectioners') sugar

100 g (3½ oz) unsalted
  butter, softened

250 g (9 oz) cream cheese,
  chilled

1 teaspoon Pimm's

zest of 1 orange

TO DECORATE

whole strawberries

orange wedges

mint sprigs

thin cucumber slices

Meanwhile, make the icing. Add the ingredients to a bowl or a stand mixer and beat together until smooth.

Place the cooled cake on a serving plate or stand, spread with the icing and decorate with whole strawberries, orange wedges, mint sprigs and cucumber slices.

—

CUKE CROOKS

Curled or 'crooked' cucumbers mostly occur due to poor pollination. To counter this, grow yours in a sunny, well-composted spot with access to bees (lavender and borage are excellent lures). As an added precaution, use a simple teepee trellis to give your cucumbers adequate space and airflow to dangle downwards while growing.

—

MORNING FRESH

Most mint varieties are spreading edibles used as sweet-smelling ground cover. They love moist soil so proximity to a pond is a particularly ideal postcode. Alternatively, for a good indoor waterside position, try placing one in a shallow pot at the foot of a sunny shower cubicle.

Beetroot and rose truffle

This recipe will become your secret weapon chocolate cake. Earthy baby beetroots are roasted until juicy to lend a dense, fudge-like texture to an already deep, dark chocolate base. The real highlight, though, is the addictive beetroot and rose truffles dusted in cocoa, which happen to be a cinch to make. Just try not to scoff them before you decorate your cake.

SERVES 8–10

10 baby beetroot (beets) (about 1.5 kg/3 lb 5 oz)

60 ml (2 fl oz/¼ cup) extra-virgin olive oil

340 g (12 oz) unsalted butter

370 g (13 oz/2 cups) soft brown sugar

340 g (12 oz/1½ cups) caster (superfine) sugar

4 large eggs

2 teaspoons vanilla extract

a few drops of rosewater, to taste

600 g (1 lb 5 oz/4 cups) plain (all-purpose) flour

4 teaspoons baking powder

160 g (5½ oz/1⅓ cups) Dutch (unsweetened) cocoa powder

4 teaspoons salt

625 g (1 lb 6 oz/2½ cups) sour cream

BEETROOT AND ROSE TRUFFLES

3 beetroot (about 150 g/5½ oz)

1 tablespoon extra-virgin olive oil

400 g (14 oz) good-quality dark chocolate (approx. 60% cocoa solids), broken into chunks

400 ml (13½ fl oz) thick (double/heavy) cream

40 g (1½ oz/1 cup) edible dried rose petals, plus extra to decorate

a few drops of rosewater

100 g (3½ oz) Dutch (unsweetened) cocoa powder

This recipe makes one tier with two layers. To pump up the tiers and recreate the cake tower pictured, as a guide you'll need to quadruple the ingredients; as well as a 20 cm (8 in) cake tin, you'll need one 23 cm (9 in) and one 25 cm (10 in) cake tin.

Preheat the oven to 175°C (345°F). Lightly grease and line two 20 cm (8 in) round cake tins with baking paper.

Toss the whole beetroot in the oil. Wrap each one separately in aluminium foil. Roast 1 hour or until soft, then remove from the oven and cool. Once cool, peel off the skin and finely grate. Set aside.

To make the truffles, cook the beetroot as per the method above, then add to a blender or food processor and blitz to a fine purée. Transfer to a saucepan set over a low heat for 2–3 minutes (this will dry up any excess moisture and help bring out the flavour, so don't skip this step). Remove from the heat and set aside.

Place the chocolate pieces in a heatproof dish. Bring the cream to the boil in a heavy-based saucepan, reduce the heat to a simmer, add half the dried rose petals and cook gently for 15 minutes, or until the flavour of the rose petals has fully infused into the cream. Strain the cream over the chocolate pieces and stir slowly until melted and glossy, then add 110 g (4 oz/¾ cup) of the beetroot purée and the rosewater and mix well. Refrigerate for 1 hour until firm. Once set, take teaspoons of the mixture and shape them into bite-sized balls, then roll them in the cocoa powder and the remaining dried rose petals to coat. Transfer to the refrigerator and leave to chill until needed.

Cream the butter and sugars together in a bowl using a hand-held mixer, or a stand mixer fitted with the paddle attachment, until light and fluffy. Beat in the eggs, vanilla and rosewater and mix in half the flour, baking powder, cocoa powder and salt. Stir in the sour cream, then mix in the remainder of the dry ingredients before gently folding in 300 g (10½ oz/1½ cups) of the grated roast beetroot until well combined (save the rest for the icing).

Continued on following page →

BEETROOT AND ROSE TRUFFLE

BEETROOT ICING

3 tablespoons finely grated roast beetroot (see method)

225 g (8 oz) unsalted butter, softened

225 g (8 oz) cream cheese, softened

500–625 g (1 lb 2 oz–1 lb 6 oz/4–5 cups) icing (confectioners') sugar

½ teaspoon vanilla extract

50 ml (1¾ fl oz) milk

Pour the batter evenly into the prepared tins and bake for 35 minutes, or until a skewer inserted into the centres comes out clean. Remove from the oven and leave to cool slightly in the tins for 5 minutes, then carefully turn out onto a wire rack and leave to cool completely.

To make the icing, beat all the ingredients together in a bowl using a hand-held mixer or a stand mixer until well combined.

Place one of the cooled cakes on a serving plate or stand and spread with half the icing. Place the second cake on top and spread with the remaining icing. To decorate, top with the truffles and scatter over a few more dried rose petals or team the truffles up with fresh garden roses.

—

BEETROOTS ARE TEAM PLAYERS

Just like radishes and carrots, beetroot's growing style helps break up and aerate soil, which lets more nutrients reach the roots of neighbouring vegetable patch friends. Members of the cabbage family will be most grateful.

Raspberry, orange and basil oil

MAKES 1 LOAF

15 g (¼ oz/1 cup) basil leaves

100 ml (3½ fl oz) extra-virgin olive oil

150 g (5½ oz) unsalted butter

zest of 1 orange

220 g (8 oz/1 cup) raw (demerara) sugar

3 eggs

25 ml (¾ fl oz) orange juice

100 ml (3½ fl oz) milk

300 g (10½ oz/2 cups) plain (all-purpose) flour

1 teaspoon baking powder

pinch of salt

185 g (6½ oz/1⅓ cups) fresh raspberries

Preheat the oven to 175°C (345°F). Lightly grease and line a 450 g (1 lb) loaf (bar) tin with baking paper.

In a bowl, blitz together the basil and oil using a hand-held blender until smooth. Add the butter, orange zest and sugar and cream together for at least 6 minutes, or until light and fluffy. Beat in the eggs one by one, then gently fold in the orange juice, milk, flour, baking powder and salt to form a batter.

Continuing to fold gently, drop the raspberries into the batter in small handfuls until evenly distributed (try not to break the raspberries up at this stage as the batter will turn a grey/purple colour rather than the vibrant pistachio green it should be).

Pour the batter into the prepared tin and bake for 1 hour, or until a skewer inserted into the centre comes out clean. Remove from the oven and leave to cool slightly in the tin for 5 minutes, then carefully turn out onto a wire rack and leave to cool completely.

—

BUG OFF

A tip for all the arachnophobes out there: try planting some basil around the entrance to your home. The scent of this herb is a big deterrent to eight-legged furry things, as well as mosquitoes. Win-win.

Pale green in appearance and with the lightest of crumbs, this loaf is modestly sweet and so moreish. The bolt of sharpness that comes from the raspberries is masked by a twist of orange and glugs of basil-flavoured olive oil.

Heirloom carrot and pumpkin

Your typical carrot cake gets an upgrade. I've swapped out the walnuts for hazelnuts, added a dash of hazelnut oil and cloves and included grated pumpkin to lend it a sweeter edge. I like to make use of heirloom carrots for their colourful looks.

SERVES 10–12

6 cloves

300 g (10½ oz/1½ cups) soft brown sugar

250 ml (8½ fl oz/1 cup) grapeseed oil

50 ml (1¾ fl oz) hazelnut oil

3 eggs

300 g (10½ oz/2 cups) plain (all-purpose) flour

1 teaspoon finely grated fresh ginger

1 teaspoon freshly grated nutmeg

1 teaspoon baking powder

1 teaspoon bicarbonate of soda (baking soda)

½ teaspoon salt

½ teaspoon vanilla extract

200 g (7 oz) heirloom carrots, grated

100 g (3½ oz) butternut pumpkin (squash), grated

280 g (10 oz/2 cups) hazelnuts, skins removed and roughly chopped

CREAM CHEESE ICING (OPTIONAL)

600 g (1 lb 5 oz) icing (confectioners') sugar

100 g (3½ oz) unsalted butter, softened

250 g (9 oz) cream cheese, chilled

Preheat the oven to 175°C (345°F). Lightly grease and line a 22 cm (9 in) round cake tin with baking paper.

In a food processor or spice grinder, blitz the cloves to form a powder. Set aside.

Beat the sugar, oils and eggs together in a large bowl using a hand-held mixer, or a stand mixer fitted with the paddle attachment, until well combined, then slowly add the flour, ginger, nutmeg, cloves, baking powder, bicarbonate of soda, salt and vanilla and mix together to form a smooth batter.

Stir the grated vegetables and half the chopped hazelnuts into the batter using a wooden spoon to incorporate evenly, then pour into the prepared tin and bake for 25–30 minutes, or until a skewer inserted into the centre comes out clean.

While the cake is baking, make the icing, if using. Add all the ingredients to a bowl or a stand mixer and beat together until smooth.

Remove the cake from the oven and leave to cool slightly in the tin for 5 minutes, then carefully turn out onto a wire rack and leave to cool completely. Spread over the icing, if using, and top with the remaining chopped hazelnuts.

—

LASAGNE COMPOST

This recipe will leave you with lots of left-over vegetable peel, so give your soil a feast. Dig a generous hole and lay down a few wet pages of newspaper, then top this with a layer of vegetable peel and then a layer of dry debris, like pea straw or dry leaves. Repeat the layering three or four times, finishing with the dry debris. Step back and let mother nature decompose your lasagne into primo earth. If you can, leave 6 months for the soil to become rich and full of earthworms.

The vines

Two tropical climbers tangle together in this simple-to-make, balmy syrup cake. A tangy dessert for when the weather warms up.

SERVES 10–12

110 g (4 oz) unsalted butter

160 g (5½ oz) caster (superfine) sugar

10 g (¼ oz/½ cup) jasmine petals

1 teaspoon thyme leaves

2 eggs

60 ml (2 fl oz/¼ cup) passionfruit pulp (about 6–8 passionfruit)

70 g (2½ oz) Greek-style yoghurt

150 g (5½ oz/1 cup) plain (all-purpose) flour

1½ teaspoons baking powder

generous pinch of salt

JASMINE AND PASSIONFRUIT SYRUP

6 jasmine flowers

125 ml (4 fl oz/½ cup) passionfruit pulp (about 12–16 passionfruit)

125 ml (4 fl oz/½ cup) water

230 g (8 oz/1 cup) caster (superfine) sugar

Preheat the oven to 180° (350°F). Lightly grease and line a 22 cm (9 in) round cake tin with baking paper.

To make the syrup, bring all the ingredients to the boil in a heavy-based saucepan, then reduce the heat and simmer gently, stirring occasionally, until the sugar dissolves completely. Remove from the heat and leave to steep while you get on with baking the cake.

Beat the butter, sugar, jasmine petals and thyme together in a bowl with an electric mixer on high speed until light and fluffy. Beat in the eggs one at a time followed by the passionfruit pulp and yoghurt, then fold in the flour, baking powder and salt and gently mix everything together to form a batter.

Pour the batter into the prepared tin and bake for 40 minutes, or until a skewer inserted into the centre comes out clean. Remove from the oven and leave to cool slightly in the tin for 5 minutes, then carefully turn out onto a wire rack and leave to cool completely.

Remove the jasmine flowers from the syrup and discard, then return the syrup to the stove top and reheat until warm. Prick your warm cake all over with a fork and ladle over the syrup evenly. Serve warm or cold.

—

A FANCY TERM FOR A TIDY TECHNIQUE

To 'espalier' a plant is to train it to grow flat against a surface. While the formal way involves real skill and patience, most climbing vines can be informally espaliered by tucking in the shooters through the trellis as the plant grows.

Corny

'I love sweetcorn. Popcorn, corn on the cob, all types of corn,' said Rick. 'Make a sweetcorn cake for me'. And so I did. This cake uses every part of the corn cob. Although the cake is delicious served on its own, the effort involved in making the corn custard cream and popcorn petal praline is worth every bite.

SERVES 10–12

3 corn cobs, with husks intact

340 g (12 oz) unsalted butter, plus extra for roasting

250 ml (8½ fl oz/1 cup) milk

230 g (8 oz/1 cup) caster (superfine) sugar

6 large eggs

150 g (5½ oz/1 cup) polenta

300 g (10½ oz/2 cups) plain (all-purpose) flour

4 teaspoons baking powder

1 teaspoon salt

This recipe makes a single-layer cake, but you can replicate the cake pictured by doubling the quantities to make two cakes. Use the corn custard cream between the layers and to ice the top and sides of the cake.

Preheat the oven to 175°C (345°F). Lightly grease and line a 22 cm (9 in) round cake tin with baking paper.

Arrange the corn cobs in their husks in a roasting tin, dotting each with a knob of butter and covering the tin with aluminium foil. Bake for 30 minutes, then remove from the oven and peel off the husks to reveal the tender cobs.

Reserving the cobs, return the husks to the tin, increase the oven temperature to 200°C (400°F) and roast the husks until browned and crispy around the edges (be careful not to burn them). Once cooked, transfer the husks to a saucepan with the milk and bring to the boil, then reduce the heat to low and simmer gently for 2–3 minutes. Take off the heat and leave the husks to steep in the milk while you prepare the rest of the cake.

When the corn cobs are cool to the touch, use a sharp knife to cut the kernels (be sure to reserve one of the cobs after cutting off the kernels – you'll need this for the corn custard). In a bowl, blitz the kernels to a rough purée using a hand-held blender, then pass the purée through a fine-mesh sieve to extract 250 ml (8 fl oz/1 cup) of corn juice.

Strain the infused husk milk, reserving 250 ml (8½ fl oz/1 cup) of the liquid. Beat the butter and sugar together in a bowl using a hand-held mixer, or a stand mixer fitted with the paddle attachment, until light and fluffy. Add the eggs one at a time followed by the polenta, flour, baking powder and salt.

Stir through the husk milk and 125 ml (4 fl oz/½ cup) of the corn juice, then pour the batter into the prepared tin and bake for 30 minutes, or until a skewer inserted into the centre comes out clean.

Continued on following page →

CORNY

CORN CUSTARD CREAM

4 egg yolks

50 g (1¾ oz /¼ cup) caster (superfine) sugar

1½ tablespoons cornflour (cornstarch)

375 ml (12½ fl oz/1½ cups) pouring cream

125 ml (4 fl oz/½ cup) corn juice (see method)

1 vanilla bean, split lengthways and seeds scraped

4 tablespoons popped popcorn

1 cooked corn cob, kernels removed (see method)

250 g (9 oz) mascarpone

POPCORN PETAL PRALINE

230 g (8 oz/1 cup) caster (superfine) sugar

60 ml (2 fl oz/¼ cup) water

2 tablespoons popped popcorn, crushed

20 g (¾ oz/1 cup) edible flower petals

Remove from the oven and leave to cool slightly in the tin for 5 minutes, then carefully turn out onto a wire rack and leave to cool completely.

To make the corn custard cream, whisk together the egg yolks, sugar and cornflour in a bowl until well combined and free of lumps. Set aside. In a saucepan, bring the cream, corn juice, vanilla bean and seeds, popcorn and the reserved corn cob to a gentle boil, then remove from the heat and strain over the egg mixture, discarding the vanilla bean and corn cob. Whisk until smooth, then pour the custard mixture into the saucepan and simmer for 3 minutes or until thickened. Pour into a bowl and leave to chill in the refrigerator, then stir through the mascarpone to combine.

To make the popcorn petal praline, roll out a sheet of baking paper on a heatproof work surface or a large chopping board. Add the sugar and water to a saucepan over a low heat and stir to dissolve, then bring to the boil. Simmer for 10 minutes, or until dark golden in colour, then remove the pan from the heat and pour the praline over your prepared surface. Scatter the popcorn and edible flowers over the surface while it's still sticky and leave for 10 minutes, or until completely set. Once set, tap the centre of the praline firmly with a sharp knife to shatter it into rough shards.

Serve each cake slice with a dollop of corn custard cream and a generous praline shard.

—
POPCORN ON THE COB
This is a really fun, freaky looking snack. To enjoy, air-dry your fresh picked cobs for 2–3 weeks by hanging them in a dry, cool area with good airflow (if you're patient) or oven-dry them on a low temperature for around 6 hours. Once your kernels are ready, slather the whole cob in butter and heat it in a covered pan until the popping spectacle is complete.

Garden lamington

An Australian classic, super-sized with a floral wallop. From a tangy hibiscus and strawberry jam to a dukkah made with macadamia nuts, toasted coconut, seeds and dried flower petals, this old-fashioned recipe has been given some thoroughly modern updates. Wattleseed is an Australian native ingredient with burnt coffee notes. If you're unable to source it, simply substitute it for good-quality instant coffee granules instead.

SERVES 10–12

125 g (4½ oz/1 cup) Dutch (unsweetened) cocoa powder

3 tablespoons wattleseed

250 ml (8½ fl oz/1 cup) boiling water

225 g (8 oz) unsalted butter

185 g (6½ oz/1 cup) soft brown sugar

230 g (8 oz/1 cup) caster (superfine) sugar

1 vanilla bean, split lengthways and seeds scraped

4 eggs

450 g (1 lb/3 cups) plain (all-purpose) flour

2 teaspoons bicarbonate of soda (baking soda)

½ teaspoon baking powder

1 teaspoon sea salt flakes

250 g (9 oz/1 cup) Greek-style yoghurt

HIBISCUS AND STRAWBERRY JAM

100 g (3½ oz) wild hibiscus, fresh or preserved

350 g (12½ oz/2⅓ cups) fresh strawberries, hulled

285 g (10 oz/1¼ cups) caster (superfine) sugar

1 teaspoon unsalted butter

juice of ½ lemon

Preheat the oven to 180°C (350°F). Lightly grease and line two 20 cm (8 in) square cake tins with baking paper.

Add the cocoa powder, wattleseed and boiling water to a bowl and stir together to form a thick paste.

Cream the butter, sugars and vanilla seeds together in a bowl with a hand-held mixer, or in a stand mixer fitted with the paddle attachment, until light and fluffy. Mix in the eggs one at a time followed by half the flour, bicarbonate of soda, baking powder and salt. Stir in the yoghurt, then add the remaining dry ingredients together with the cocoa and wattleseed paste and mix to form a batter.

Divide the batter evenly between the prepared tins and bake for 45 minutes, or until a skewer inserted into the centres comes out clean. Remove from the oven and leave to cool slightly in the tins for 5 minutes, then carefully turn out onto a wire rack and leave to cool completely.

While the cakes are cooling, make the jam. Add the hibiscus, strawberries and sugar to a deep-sided saucepan and bring to the boil, stirring continuously. Reduce the heat to medium, then add the butter and lemon juice and simmer for 10–15 minutes, or until the mixture has thickened enough to coat the back of a spoon. Remove from the heat and set aside to cool.

FUDGE ICING

600 g (1 lb 5 oz) icing
  (confectioners') sugar

200 g (7 oz) unsalted butter

80 g (2¾ oz/⅔ cup) Dutch
  (unsweetened) cocoa
  powder

80 ml (2½ fl oz/⅓ cup) milk

FLORAL DUKKAH

160 g (5½ oz/1 cup)
  macadamia nuts

120 g (4½ oz/2 cups)
  shredded coconut

40 g (1½ oz/¼ cup) sesame
  seeds

80 g (2¾ oz/½ cup) pine nuts

5 g (¼ oz/¼ cup) dried
  flower petals

To make the fudge icing, beat all the ingredients together in a bowl or in a stand mixer until the mixture is light and fluffy.

For the floral dukkah, add the macadamia nuts to a large frying pan set over a medium–high heat and toast, stirring often, until lightly browned. Remove from the heat and leave to cool, then finely chop. Toast the shredded coconut, sesame seeds and pine nuts in the same manner and leave to cool, then mix together well with the chopped macadamia nuts and dried flower petals. Set aside.

Once cool, use a sharp knife to trim off the top of each cake so that the two are of equal height. Spread a generous layer of jam evenly over one of the cakes, then place the second cake on top. Spread the top and sides of the layered cake with the icing and gently press the dukkah mixture evenly over the cake to coat completely.

—

NO-NOSE ROSE

While hibiscus flowers lend vivid colour and a cranberry-like flavour to dishes, please don't plant them for their perfume, because they have none.

Smoked tarragon locket

I had a very special grandma named Lucy Locket. She was a cockney sweetheart and an absolute fiend for sweets — custard éclairs, bite-sized fudge pieces and slabs of sticky toffee were her weaknesses. This is her recipe for 'the ultimate chocolate cake'. It's a light, springy chocolate cake pockmarked with toffee dimples and edges. I've added my own touch by smoking the flour and cocoa with home-dried tarragon to give the cake a subtle liquorice, tobacco and vanilla background. Serve it to your granny and tell me what she thinks.

SERVES 10–12

375 g (13 oz/2½ cups) self-raising flour

30 g (1 oz/¼ cup) Dutch (unsweetened) cocoa powder

5 g (¼ oz/¼ cup) dried tarragon

1 teaspoon bicarbonate of soda (baking soda)

230 g (8 oz/1 cup) caster (superfine) sugar

60 ml (2 fl oz/¼ cup) golden syrup

2 eggs

200 ml (7 fl oz) grapeseed oil

200 ml (7 fl oz) milk

1 large handful tarragon sprigs, to decorate

CHOCOLATE ICING

125 g (4½ oz) unsalted butter

130 g (4½ oz) milk chocolate, broken into small chunks

185 g (6½ oz/1½ cups) icing (confectioners') sugar

60 ml (2 fl oz/¼ cup) milk

Preheat the oven to 175°C (345°F). Lightly grease and line a 22 cm (9 in) heart-shaped or round cake tin with baking paper.

Add the flour and cocoa to a mixing bowl and stir to combine. Cover the bowl with plastic wrap. Add the tarragon to the burn chamber of a smoking gun and smoke the flour mixture according to the manufacturer's instructions, being sure to only do this for a few seconds so as not to overdo the tarragon fragrance.

Sift the smoked flour mixture into a large mixing bowl together with the bicarbonate of soda and caster sugar. Beat in the golden syrup, eggs, oil and milk for 3 minutes, or until well combined, then pour the batter into the prepared tin and bake for 1 hour, or until a skewer inserted into the centre comes out clean. Remove from the oven and leave to cool slightly in the tin for 5 minutes, then carefully turn out onto a wire rack and leave to cool completely.

While the cake is cooling, make the icing. Place the butter and chocolate in a heatproof bowl set over a saucepan of lightly simmering water and melt gently, stirring, until completely smooth. Remove from the heat, stir in the icing sugar and milk and beat until the mixture is smooth and glossy.

Place the cooled cake on a serving plate or stand and spread the top and sides with the chocolate icing. Decorate with the tarragon sprigs.

—

THE FRENCH DO IT BETTER

Tarragon is a woody creeping plant with three main varieties — Russian, Mexican and French. While Russian and Mexican varieties are bushier in looks and coarser in texture, French tarragon is considered to have the truest and softest flavour of the three. Plant yours from cuttings in sandy soil within reach of full sunlight.

—

SMOKING GUN
You'll need a smoking gun to complete this recipe as it stands, but if you don't have this sort of equipment then keep it traditional and enjoy my nan's original version.

Peach and pickled petal

A homely bite with fresh cut peaches nestled in a deep den of mascarpone and soft brown sugar, and served with a perky side of sweet-and-sour rose petals. If you can, try to make the pickled petals at least a week ahead of time. The longer you steep them, the more complex they'll taste.

MAKES 12

250 g (9 oz) unsalted butter

1 teaspoon vanilla extract

110 g (4 oz/½ cup) raw (demerara) sugar

95 g (3¼ oz/½ cup) soft brown sugar

3 eggs

250 g (9 oz) mascarpone, chilled

300 g (10½ oz/2 cups) plain (all-purpose) flour

1 teaspoon baking powder

1 teaspoon bicarbonate of soda (baking soda)

pinch of salt

3 very ripe peaches, quartered and stones removed

PICKLED PETALS

20 g (1 oz/1 cup) rose petals

250 g (9 oz) sugar

250 ml (8½ fl oz/1 cup) apple-cider vinegar

To make the pickled petals, wash and drain the rose petals and place them in a sterilised glass jar. Add the sugar and vinegar to a saucepan and bring to the boil, then reduce the heat and simmer, stirring gently, until the sugar dissolves. Pour the hot liquid over the petals, seal the jar and leave to pickle for at least 1 week.

When ready to bake, preheat the oven to 175°C (345°F). Lightly grease a 12-hole standard muffin tin or loaf tin.

Cream the butter, vanilla and sugars together in a bowl using a hand-held mixer, or a stand mixer fitted with the paddle attachment, until light and fluffy. Beat in the eggs one by one, followed by 150 g (5½ oz) of the mascarpone. Fold in the flour, baking powder, bicarbonate of soda and salt to form a batter.

Divide the batter mixture evenly among the muffin tin holes and top each with a peach quarter. Bake for 45 minutes, or until a skewer inserted into the centre of a muffin comes out clean. Remove from the oven and leave to cool slightly in the tin for 5 minutes, then transfer to a wire rack and leave to cool completely.

Once cool, top each muffin with a dollop of the remaining mascarpone and a pinch of the pickled petals to finish.

—

SPOTTED ROSE

Banish black spot fungus from your roses by making use of every cake maker's staple: bicarbonate of soda. Mix together 1½ teaspoons bicarb with ⅓ teaspoon dishwashing detergent and 1 litre (34 fl oz/4 cups) water, then spray the mixture onto your roses once a week until the disease has disappeared.

Honey for Ray

SERVES 6–8

3 tablespoons ground lemon myrtle (or lemon thyme or lemon balm)

3 tablespoons fennel seeds

500 g (1 lb 2 oz) unsalted butter

330 g (11½ oz/1½ cups) raw (demerara) sugar

6 eggs

250 ml (8½ fl oz/1 cup) milk

600 g (1 lb 5 oz/4 cups) plain (all-purpose) flour

4 teaspoons baking powder

½ teaspoon salt

80 g (2¾ oz/½ cup) finely grated fennel

HONEY SYRUP

125 ml (4 fl oz/½ cup) freshly squeezed lemon juice

500 ml (17 fl oz/2 cups) honey

375 ml (12½ fl oz/1½ cups) water

HONEY ICING

4 teaspoons honey

600 g (1 lb 5 oz) icing (confectioners') sugar

100 g (3½ oz) unsalted butter, softened

250 g (9 oz) cream cheese, chilled

This recipe makes one tier with two layers. To create the cake pictured, as a guide you'll need to triple the ingredients; as well as a 20 cm (8 in) cake tin, you'll need one 23 cm (9 in) and one 25 cm (10 in) cake tin.

Preheat the oven to 175°C (345°F). Lightly grease and line two 20 cm (8 in) round cake tins with baking paper.

Toast the lemon myrtle and fennel seeds together in a saucepan over a medium heat until fragrant. Remove from the heat, transfer to a large mixing bowl and leave to cool completely.

Once cooled, add the butter and sugar to the bowl with the toasted lemon myrtle and fennel seeds and cream together for 2–3 minutes or until light and fluffy. Add the eggs one at a time and continue to beat until incorporated. Stir in the milk, then sift over the flour, baking powder and salt and fold together to form a batter.

Using your hands, squeeze the grated fennel to remove any excess moisture, then add it to the batter and stir together gently to distribute evenly. Divide the batter evenly between the prepared tins and bake for 1 hour, or until a skewer inserted into the centres comes out clean.

Meanwhile, make the honey syrup. Combine all the ingredients in a saucepan set over a medium-high heat and stir together until the honey dissolves. Bring to the boil, then remove from the heat. Set aside.

While the cakes are hot and in their tins, prick the tops with a fork and ladle over 250 ml (8½ fl oz/1 cup) of the honey syrup. Cool on a wire rack.

To make the honey icing, beat all the ingredients together in a bowl using a hand-held mixer, or a stand mixer fitted with the paddle attachment, until smooth.

Place one of the cooled cakes on a serving plate or stand and spread with half the icing, then place the second cake on top. Spread over the remaining icing and serve with the remaining honey syrup.

—

A PERENNIAL THAT KEEPS GIVING

You can eat every part of the fennel plant. The bulbs and feathery fronds are the most consumed parts, but once your fennel has 'bolted' you can also use the yellow flowers and seeds as edibles, or collect the fennel pollen. To do this, bundle together some freshly cut flower heads, cover with a paper bag and tie it closed, then turn the bags upside down and shake the pollen loose. Once the flower heads on your plant start to dry out, use the same technique to collect the seeds.

—

LEMON MYRTLE

This is an Australian native ingredient with subtle eucalyptus notes. It can be substituted with lemon balm or lemon thyme.

This one goes out to my baby boy. He was two months old when I wrote this recipe and I like to think it will become his most requested afternoon treat. The combination of lemon myrtle, fennel and honey syrup creates a creamy, floral finish. I like to decorate this cake with Australian native flora and eucalyptus, and a handful of crumbled shortbread. It's soft and lush, just like Ray Lou.

Sweet snacks

Rhubarb, basil and oatmeal slice

This is basically hand-held rhubarb crumble, which makes me very happy. Stow one away in your pocket for your next wintry stroll, or stay cosy at home and serve them with clotted cream and a generous handful of fruity, torn basil.

MAKES 6

115 g (4 oz) unsalted butter

200 g (7 oz) soft brown sugar

1 large egg

2 teaspoons vanilla extract

225 g (8 oz/1½ cups) plain (all-purpose) flour

½ teaspoon bicarbonate of soda (baking soda)

¼ teaspoon salt

170 g (6 oz/1¾ cups) rolled oats

1 handful fresh torn basil leaves

RHUBARB COMPOTE

450 g (1 lb) rhubarb stalks, cut into 3 cm (1¼ in) pieces

100 g (3½ oz) caster (superfine) sugar

2 teaspoons balsamic vinegar

1 teaspoon vanilla extract

Preheat the oven to 180°C (350°F). Lightly grease and line a 20 cm (8 in) square cake tin with baking paper.

To make the rhubarb compote, add all the ingredients to a saucepan, cover with a lid and bring to the boil over a medium–high heat. Reduce the heat to low and simmer gently for 15–20 minutes, or until the rhubarb has softened and the mixture is nice and thick. Remove from the heat and set aside.

Beat together the butter and brown sugar in a bowl using a hand-held mixer, or a stand mixer fitted with the paddle attachment, until light and fluffy. Beat in the egg and vanilla followed by the flour, bicarbonate of soda, salt and oats to form a dough.

Press two-thirds of the dough into the base of the prepared tin. Spoon over the rhubarb compote to cover evenly, then crumble over the remaining dough. Bake for 25–30 minutes, or until lightly browned. Remove from the oven and leave to cool in the tin, then cut into slices. Sprinkle over a little torn basil to decorate before serving.

—

THROUGH THE GRAPEVINE

A common garden tale is that rhubarb leaves contain a substance that will repel insects. Boil the rhubarb leaves in water to produce a colourful home-made insecticide and fight off everyday garden pests.

Hibiscus and cherry brownies with coconut caramel

MAKES 12

285 g (10 oz) good-quality dark chocolate (approx. 60% cocoa solids), broken into chunks

115 g (4 oz) unsalted butter

240 g (8½ oz) raw (demerara) sugar

2 teaspoons vanilla extract

2 large eggs

1 teaspoon ground cinnamon

½ teaspoon freshly ground star anise

¼ teaspoon freshly ground cloves

240 g (8½ oz) plain (all-purpose) flour

¼ teaspoon salt

Dutch (unsweetened) cocoa powder, for dusting (optional)

HIBISCUS AND CHERRY SOAK

25 g (1 oz/1 cup) hibiscus petals, fresh or preserved

300 g (10½ oz/2 cups) morello cherries, pitted

500 ml (17 fl oz/2 cups) red wine

250 ml (8½ fl oz/1 cup) sherry

1 cinnamon stick

3 star anise, whole

COCONUT CARAMEL SAUCE

125 ml (4 fl oz/½ cup) coconut milk

1 tablespoon light corn syrup

220 g (8 oz/1 cup) coconut sugar

60 ml (2 fl oz/¼ cup) water

60 g (2 oz) unsalted butter, at room temperature

Preheat the oven to 175°C (345°F). Grease and line a 30 × 20 cm (12 × 8 in) brownie tin with baking paper.

For the hibiscus and cherry soak, bring all the ingredients to the boil in a heavy-based saucepan. Reduce the heat to medium–low and simmer gently for 10 minutes, then remove from the heat, transfer to a container and leave to steep for a minimum of 1 hour, ideally overnight.

When ready to bake, gently melt the chocolate and butter in a heatproof bowl set over a saucepan of lightly simmering water, stirring until completely smooth. Remove from the heat and leave to cool until lukewarm, then whisk in the sugar, vanilla and eggs until evenly combined. Remove the cherries and petals from the steeping liquid and fold them gently into the brownie mixture together with the spices, flour and salt to form a batter.

Pour the batter into the prepared tin and bake for 20 minutes, or until set on the surface and lightly puffed up around the edges (this will give you the nice, gooey centre you are after here – so be sure not to over-bake!).

While the brownies are baking, make the coconut caramel sauce. Warm the coconut milk in a small heavy-based saucepan set over a low heat. In a separate saucepan, whisk together the corn syrup, coconut sugar and water over a medium heat. Continue to whisk until the sugar is completely dissolved, then bring to the boil. Leave to bubble and froth up for 2–3 minutes, then reduce the heat to low and carefully pour over the warm coconut milk. Add the butter and whisk to combine, then remove from the heat and leave to cool slightly.

Remove the brownies from the oven and leave to cool in the tin, then cut into pieces. Dust with a little cocoa powder, if you like, and pour over the coconut caramel sauce to serve.

—

THINK TROPICAL

With varieties including Flamenco, Chiffon Breeze and Long Tan, hibiscus plants should be given the island treatment they deserve. Plant them in warm conditions in northerly light and water regularly for best results.

Unapologetically indulgent, these fudgy, boozy brownies are drenched in a caramel ode to the tropics. If you can, soak the hibiscus and cherries in wine for as long as possible. Then, save the strained liquid to make a fruity sangria reward.

Green and white cookies

NYC's famous black and white cookies get a garden makeover. These cake-like cookies are iced with an apple blossom rocket ganache on one side and a traditional lemon icing on the other. Carry them straight to the coffee table for a chorus of 'oooohs'.

MAKES 16

15 g (½ oz/¼ cup) English spinach, stems removed

1 teaspoon vanilla extract

170 g (6 oz) unsalted butter

230 g (8 oz/1 cup) caster (superfine) sugar

2 eggs

125 ml (4 fl oz/½ cup) buttermilk

375 g (13 oz/2½ cups) plain (all-purpose) flour

1 teaspoon bicarbonate of soda (baking soda)

1 teaspoon salt

APPLE BLOSSOM ROCKET GANACHE

10 g (¼ oz/½ cup) apple blossoms, plus extra to decorate (optional)

85 ml (2¾ fl oz) thick (double/heavy) cream

20 g (¾ oz/1 cup) rocket (arugula), finely chopped

225 g (8 oz) white chocolate, broken into chunks

4 teaspoons milk powder

Preheat the oven to 175°C (345°F). Line a baking tray with baking paper.

Blanch the spinach in a saucepan of boiling water for 1 minute. Drain and leave to cool, then finely chop.

Add the blanched spinach, vanilla and 70 g (2½ oz) of the butter to a bowl and blitz using a hand-held mixer until combined. Transfer the green butter to the bowl of a stand mixer fitted with the paddle attachment together with the sugar and remaining butter and beat on high speed until voluminous, about 6 minutes. Beat in the eggs one by one, then gently fold in the buttermilk, flour, bicarbonate of soda and salt to form a batter.

Scoop out tablespoons of the batter and dollop them onto the prepared baking tray, leaving around 5 cm (2 in) between each mound of batter to allow for spreading. With slightly wet fingers, pat and shape the batter mounds into circles, then transfer to the oven and bake for 15 minutes or until lightly golden around the edges. Remove from the oven and leave to cool slightly on the tray for 5 minutes before transferring to a wire rack to cool completely.

While the cookies are cooling, make the ganache. Add the apple blossoms and cream to a heavy-based saucepan and bring to the boil, then remove from the heat and set aside to steep. Blanch the rocket in 250 ml (8½ fl oz/1 cup) boiling water until tender and bright green, then drain and push the warm rocket through a fine-mesh sieve to draw out a green water. Strain the infused cream into a bowl set over a saucepan of lightly simmering water, discarding the blossoms. Add the white chocolate and 40 ml (1¼ fl oz) of the rocket water and melt gently over a medium heat, stirring, until completely smooth. Whisk in the milk powder to combine.

Continued on following page →

LEMON ICING

185 g (6½ oz/1½ cups) icing (confectioners') sugar

4 teaspoons light corn syrup

2 teaspoons freshly squeezed lemon juice

¼ teaspoon vanilla extract

1–2 tablespoons water

Using a butter knife or a small metal spatula, spread a layer of ganache evenly over one half of each of the cooled cookies. Repeat until the ganache is thick and you can't see the cookie underneath. If you like, scatter a few apple blossom petals over the ganache-covered side of the cookies to decorate.

To make the icing, mix all the ingredients together in a bowl or in a stand mixer fitted with the paddle attachment until smooth, then spread the icing over the other half of the cookies to finish. Leave to set before serving.

—

MOSS MILKSHAKE

While you have the buttermilk out for this recipe, make your very own moss. Grab 250 ml (8½ fl oz/1 cup) of buttermilk and blitz it together with a piece of found moss, then paint the mixture around shaded areas of your garden wherever you'd like a splash of emerald — on rocks, fences, concrete planters, even tree trunks. For the first few weeks spritz your baby moss using a mister filled with equal parts buttermilk and water to keep it moist and to encourage growth.

Kale, lemon and caraway muffins

Sophisticated muffins made for grown ups, these guys are a great treat for casual hangs or as a little something special to brighten up your week.

MAKES 12

4 teaspoons caraway seeds

110 g (4 oz) unsalted butter

220 g (8 oz/1 cup) granulated sugar

4 teaspoons lemon zest

1 egg

60 ml (2 fl oz/¼ cup) freshly squeezed lemon juice

250 g (9 oz/1 cup) ricotta

300 g (10½ oz/2 cups) plain (all-purpose) flour

½ teaspoon baking powder

½ teaspoon bicarbonate of soda (baking soda)

½ teaspoon salt

70 g (2½ oz/1 cup) finely shredded kale, tough stems removed

Preheat the oven to 175°C (345°F). Line a 12-hole standard muffin tin with paper cases.

Toast the caraway seeds in a frying pan over a medium heat, tossing them gently from time to time, for 5–8 minutes until browned. Remove from the pan and set aside.

Cream the butter, sugar, lemon zest and caraway seeds together in a bowl, or in a stand mixer fitted with the paddle attachment, until light and fluffy. Beat in the egg, lemon juice and ricotta until smooth, then fold in the flour, baking powder, bicarbonate of soda, salt and kale.

Divide the batter evenly among the paper cases and bake for 20 minutes, or until a skewer inserted into the centre of a muffin comes out clean. Remove from the oven and leave to cool slightly in the tin for 5 minutes, then transfer to a wire rack and leave to cool completely.

—

NO MORE NIBBLES

Being a member of the cabbage family, kale is particularly prone to attacks from the common white cabbage moth. Netting your seedlings is one good way of preventing the moths from eating all your kale before you do — use bamboo poles or PVC piping to make a frame for your net, then hang it high enough to allow air flow and growth of your plants. Once your kale plants are established, keep your eye out for green caterpillars hiding on the underside of leaves.

Flower confetti madeleines

Just a handful of ingredients come together to make something quick and irresistible. Use whatever dried petals you have on hand, or make these madeleines your own invention and experiment with a pinch of herbs instead.

MAKES 12

5 g (¼ oz/¼ cup) dried
  flower petals

100 g (3½ oz) plain
  (all-purpose) flour

pinch of sea salt

1 teaspoon baking powder

75 g (2¾ oz) unsalted
  butter, melted and cooled

90 g (3 oz) caster
  (superfine) sugar

2 teaspoons vanilla extract

zest of 1 lemon

2 eggs

Preheat the oven to 175°C (345°F). Very lightly grease a 12-hole fluted madeleine mould.

Add the flower petals, flour, sea salt and baking powder to a bowl and mix together well.

In a separate bowl, or in a stand mixer fitted with the paddle attachment, beat together the butter, sugar, vanilla and lemon zest until light and fluffy. Beat in the eggs one by one, then gently fold in the flour mixture to form a batter.

Spoon the batter into the prepared madeleine mould and bake for 10 minutes, or until golden. Remove from the oven and give the mould a little jiggle to prise out the madeleines while still hot (they run the risk of overcooking if left in the mould). Leave to cool on a wire rack.

Lavender and bay leaf shortbread

Whip up this shortbread when you have someone important but mean coming over (think landlord or rich aunty) – you want to impress them but you don't want to kill yourself with a tricky recipe. Here the perfume of lavender is turned down and herbed up with everyone's pantry staple, the bay leaf. The result is both buttery and botanical.

MAKES 8

115 g (4 oz/½ cup) caster (superfine) sugar

3 bay leaves, stalks removed

2 teaspoons fresh or dried lavender heads, plus extra for garnish

225 g (8 oz) unsalted butter

zest of 1 lemon

225 g (8 oz/1½ cups) plain (all-purpose) flour

115 g (4 oz/¾ cup) rice flour

pinch of salt

Blitz together the sugar, bay leaves and lavender in a food processor or spice grinder to form a powder.

Setting aside 40 g (1½ oz) of the sugar powder, add the remainder together with the butter and lemon zest to a bowl, or a stand mixer fitted with the paddle attachment, and cream together until light and fluffy. Stir in the flours and salt by hand and mix gently to combine, then turn the mix out onto a clean floured work surface and knead lightly until it just comes together to form a dough. Shape the dough into a flat disc, cover it in plastic wrap and refrigerate for 30 minutes.

Preheat the oven to 175°C (345°F). Line a baking tray with baking paper.

Once chilled, roll the dough out on the floured work surface into a circle approximately 2 cm (¾ in) thick. If you like, score the dough with a sharp knife as if you were marking out wedges on a pizza (this will help you divide the shortbread into wedges later), then sprinkle it with the reserved sugar and prick it all over with a fork.

Transfer the dough to the prepared baking tray and bake for 25 minutes, or until golden brown. Remove from the oven and leave to cool slightly, then cut into wedges and transfer to a wire rack to cool completely.

—

SWEET-SMELLING FRIENDS
Evergreen lavender helps to keep aphids at a safe distance from neighbouring roses. Keep them planted together for a pest-free union.

Garden jam drops

MAKES 20

125 g (4½ oz) unsalted butter

70 g (2½ oz) icing (confectioners') sugar

1 egg yolk

45 g (1½ oz) cream cheese, chilled and diced

2 teaspoons vanilla extract

175 g (6 oz) plain (all-purpose) flour

½ teaspoon baking powder

½ teaspoon bicarbonate of soda (baking soda)

pinch of salt

approx. 200 g (7 oz) Carrot and orange marmalade (see below), Cherry geranium jam (below), Hibiscus and strawberry jam (page 106) or Cherry tomato jam (page 132)

CARROT AND ORANGE MARMALADE

200 g (7 oz) carrots, peeled and grated

250 ml (8½ fl oz/1 cup) freshly squeezed orange juice

zest of 1 orange

1 teaspoon minced fresh ginger

4 cloves

1 cinnamon stick

220 g (8 oz/1 cup) granulated sugar

225 ml (7½ fl oz) water

CHERRY GERANIUM JAM

1 kg (2 lb 3 oz) cherries, stoned

4–6 scented geranium leaves

375 ml (12½ fl oz/1½ cups) honey

juice of 1 lemon

If you are making the carrot and orange marmalade, put the carrot, orange juice and zest, ginger, cloves, cinnamon stick and sugar into a heavy-based saucepan and stir. Leave to macerate for at least 1 hour, ideally overnight. Add the water to the pan and bring to the boil, then reduce the heat to medium and simmer for 20 minutes, or until thick. To test if the jam is ready, dollop a small smear onto a chilled saucer – if it crinkles up when you push it with your finger, it's ready; if not then continue to simmer and test again in a few minutes. When the jam is ready, remove the cloves and cinnamon stick and leave to cool a little, then set aside if using straight away or spoon into sterilised jars until needed (it will keep for at least 3 months).

If you are making the cherry geranium jam, add the cherries to a sterilised jar. Place the scented geranium leaves around the inside of the jar. Warm the honey and lemon juice in a saucepan until syrupy, then pour it over the cherries. Seal the jar and transfer it to a saucepan of warm water set over a low–medium heat. Bring to the boil, then turn off the heat and leave the jar to cool down completely. Set aside until needed (the longer you leave the jam the more fragrant the geranium scent will be; ideally, leave it 24 hours).

Preheat the oven to 180°C (350°F). Line a baking tray with baking paper.

Beat the butter, icing sugar and egg yolk together in a bowl with a hand-held mixer, or in a stand mixer fitted with the paddle attachment, until light and fluffy. Add the cream cheese and vanilla and beat until the mixture is smooth, then gently fold in the flour, baking powder, bicarbonate of soda and salt.

With floured hands, divide the dough into 20 even-sized pieces and shape into small balls. Place the balls on the prepared baking tray, flatten slightly with the palm of your hand, then use your thumb to make little indents in the centre of each biscuit. Spoon 1 teaspoon of jam into each indent and bake for 10–15 minutes, or until golden.

Remove from the oven and leave to cool slightly on the tray for 5 minutes, then transfer to a wire rack and leave to cool completely.

—

ROOTY TOOT TOOT

Cinnamon is a secret weapon for crafty propagators in the know, acting as a natural rooting hormone and keeping cuttings free of disease, fungus and bacteria. Dip cuttings in freshly ground cinnamon (with a smidge of honey) and plant with confidence.

A biscuit with minimal frills but plenty of wow. I've given you four jam options here, so you can pick the right one to suit the seasons. If you'd like to save your jam for a hot crumpet, then make sure you have clean sterilised jars at the ready.

Cherry tomato turnovers
(aka fancy pop tarts)

Sweet baby tomatoes are given a jammy treatment before being stuffed into a crumbly empanada dough and dusted with tomato-skin salt to finish. Highly addictive.

MAKES 8

300 g (10½ oz/2 cups) plain (all-purpose) flour

225 g (8 oz) unsalted butter, chilled and diced

3 egg yolks

3 tablespoons sour cream

1 tablespoon freshly squeezed lemon juice

1 egg white

1 tablespoon water

250 g (9 oz/1 cup) ricotta

2 tablespoons icing (confectioner's) sugar

55 g (2 oz/¼ cup) raw caster (superfine) sugar

TOMATO SALT

5 tomatoes

1 teaspoon extra-virgin olive oil

160 g (5½ oz/½ cup) coarse sea salt

CHERRY TOMATO JAM

420 g (15 oz/3 cups) cherry tomatoes, quartered

170 g (6 oz/¾ cup) caster (superfine) sugar

Mix the flour and butter together in a bowl with your fingertips to form coarse breadcrumbs. Beat the egg yolks lightly, then add them to the bowl along with the sour cream and lemon juice and mix together to form a rough dough. Turn the dough out onto a floured work surface and knead briefly to bring it together, then divide it into eight even-sized pieces and shape into balls. Cover with plastic wrap and leave to chill for a minimum of 5 hours, ideally overnight.

Preheat the oven to 100°C (210°F).

To make the tomato salt, bring a large saucepan of water to the boil. Using a paring knife, cut a cross into the bottom of each tomato, then drop them into the boiling water and wait for the skins to start to peel back, about 1 minute. Drain the tomatoes and leave them to cool in cold water, then gently peel back the skins using the knife (reserve the tomato flesh for sauces). Pat the skins dry and drizzle over the olive oil to coat. Arrange the skins on a baking tray in an even layer and cook for 30 minutes or until crispy. Remove from the oven and leave to cool, then transfer to a pestle and mortar and crush together with the coarse sea salt. Set aside.

To make the cherry tomato jam, add the cherry tomatoes and sugar to a high-sided saucepan set over a medium–low heat. Cook for 20 minutes, stirring occasionally, until the jam is nice and thick. Remove from the heat and leave to cool.

Increase the oven temperature to 175°C (345°F).

Whisk the egg white together with the water in a small bowl to form a wash. In a separate bowl, beat the ricotta and icing sugar together until smooth.

When ready to bake, roll the chilled dough balls out to a 5mm (¼ in) thickness and cut each into an 8 cm (3¼ in) square. Spread a heaped tablespoon of the cherry tomato jam over one of the squares followed by a tablespoon of the ricotta and icing sugar mixture. Fold it over diagonally to form a triangle, then press down on the edges with a fork to seal. Repeat with the rest of the pastry squares. Using a pastry brush, lightly coat the turnovers with the egg wash and sprinkle over the raw caster sugar. Bake for 15 minutes, or until golden brown.

Remove the turnovers from the oven and leave to cool slightly on the tray. Serve warm, with a little of the tomato salt sprinkled over to finish.

—

BIRDS AND BEES
Cherry tomatoes need a little TLC to fruit, so pretend you're a bee and help pollinate your plants by giving them a sexy little shake when they're in bloom. You can even use a soft toothbrush to move the pollen from plant to plant. And while you're at it, be sure to prune any little suckers on the plants to encourage growth.

Honeysuckle brioche pie

A decadent, botanical pie with marmalade vibes. A hefty dose of honeysuckle is immersed in orange thyme and golden syrup to create a super sweet, slightly bitter bite. The filling gets mopped up in brioche crumbs, then encased in a savoury pastry and a layer of marzipan. It's true love.

SERVES 8–10

25 g (1 oz) unsalted butter

125 ml (4 fl oz/½ cup) golden syrup

60 ml (2 fl oz/¼ cup) honey

20 g (¾ oz/1 cup) honeysuckle blossoms, fresh or dried

100 g (3½ oz) marzipan, at room temperature

75 g (2¾ oz) brioche, torn into breadcrumbs

1 teaspoon orange thyme leaves

55 g (2 oz/½ cup) ground almonds

zest and juice of 1 orange

PASTRY

370 g (13 oz) unsalted butter, at room temperature

310 g (11 oz) cream cheese

1 teaspoon salt

1 teaspoon freshly squeezed lemon juice

375 g (13 oz/2½ cups) wholemeal (whole-wheat) plain flour

Preheat the oven to 200°C (400°F). Lightly grease and line a 20 cm (8 in) round pie tin with baking paper.

Melt the butter, golden syrup and honey together with the honeysuckle in a saucepan over a low heat. Stir to combine, then remove from the heat and set aside to steep.

To make the pastry, combine all the ingredients in a stand mixer fitted with the dough hook attachment and mix on medium speed until the dough just comes together, about 4 minutes. On a clean floured work surface, roll out the pastry into a circle roughly 5 mm (¼ in) thick and use it to line the base and sides of your pie tin. Prick a few times with a fork and transfer to the refrigerator for 5 minutes to rest.

Lightly dust the work surface with icing sugar, then roll out the marzipan to the same shape and thickness as the pastry. Place on top of the pastry.

Pass the syrup mixture through a sieve to remove the honeysuckle, then add the strained syrup to a bowl together with the brioche breadcrumbs, orange thyme, ground almonds, and orange zest and juice. Stir together to combine, then pour the filling into the lined tin and bake for 40 minutes, or until golden and risen.

Remove from the oven and leave to cool slightly in the tin for 5 minutes, then transfer to a wire rack and leave to cool completely.

—

A SPOOKY BLOOM

During the 1800s the British would plant honeysuckle in front of their houses to keep evil spirits and witchcraft away. The perfect edible for the superstitious.

Sweet potato rugelach

Made with creamy sweet potato, plump raisins, dark chocolate chips and a cream cheese pastry, these rugelach are a deeply satisfying treat.

MAKES 24

1 tablespoon soft brown sugar, plus extra for dusting

225 g (8 oz) unsalted butter, cut into cubes

125 g (4½ oz) cream cheese, at room temperature

185 g (6½ oz/1¼ cups) plain (all-purpose) flour

¼ teaspoon salt

1 egg yolk

1 tablespoon water

1 tablespoon caster (superfine) sugar

SWEET POTATO FILLING

60 g (2 oz/½ cup) raisins, roughly chopped

2 medium sweet potatoes, peeled and cut into cubes

1 tablespoon extra-virgin olive oil

1 teaspoon ground cinnamon

90 g (3 oz/¾ cup) icing (confectioners') sugar

45 g (1½ oz/¼ cup) dark chocolate chips

Preheat the oven to 200°C (400°F).

Put the brown sugar, butter, cream cheese, flour and salt in a large bowl and rub together with your fingertips to form coarse breadcrumbs. Knead together very briefly to make a soft dough, then divide the dough into three equal-sized pieces. Shape the dough pieces into rough discs, cover with plastic wrap and chill in the refrigerator for 1 hour.

Meanwhile, to make the filling, put the chopped raisins in a bowl, cover with boiling water and leave to soak for at least 30 minutes. Drain and set aside.

Toss the sweet potato pieces together with the oil and cinnamon to coat evenly, then transfer to a baking tray and roast for 20 minutes, or until tender. Leave to cool, then blitz to a purée with a hand-held blender.

In a bowl, stir together 400 g (14 oz/2 cups) of the purée with the icing sugar and soaked raisins until evenly combined.

Reduce the oven temperature to 170°C (340°F) and line a baking tray with baking paper.

Lightly knead the chilled dough pieces on a lightly floured surface dusted in a little brown sugar. Shape into circles approximately 5 mm (¼ in) thick and cut each into eight wedges. Using a small knife, spread the filling over each wedge and sprinkle over the dark chocolate chips. Starting from the wide ends, roll up each dough triangle towards the centre to make mini croissant shapes.

Place the rugelach on the prepared baking tray. Whisk the egg yolk and water together to form a glaze and use it to brush the rugelach, then sprinkle over the caster sugar and bake for 30 minutes until golden. Remove from the oven and leave to cool slightly before transferring to a wire rack to cool completely.

Salad sandwich cookies

MAKES 12

350 g (12½ oz) unsalted butter

60 g (2 oz/½ cup) icing (confectioners') sugar

6 marigolds, petals removed, plus extra to decorate

250 g (9 oz/1⅔ cups) plain (all-purpose) flour

60 g (2 oz/½ cup) cornflour (cornstarch)

KALE CRUMBS

3 kale leaves, tough central stems removed

1 tablespoon extra-virgin olive oil

AVOCADO BUTTERCREAM

½ avocado

75 g (2¾ oz) unsalted butter

110 g (4 oz) cream cheese

½ teaspoon vanilla extract

250 g (9 oz/2 cups) icing (confectioners') sugar

Preheat the oven to 180°C (350°F) and line two baking trays with baking paper.

For the kale crumbs, wash and dry the kale leaves and tear them into small pieces, then transfer to a bowl, drizzle over the oil and mix to coat evenly. Pat the kale pieces with paper towel to remove any excess oil, then spread them out on one of the prepared trays and bake for 15 minutes, or until crispy and brown but not burnt. Remove from the oven and leave to cool, then break into fine, crispy crumbs.

Cream the butter, icing sugar and marigold petals together in a bowl using a hand-held mixer, or a stand mixer fitted with the paddle attachment, until light and fluffy. Add the flour and cornflour and, using your hands, mix together to form a dough.

Spoon teaspoonfuls of the dough onto the remaining baking tray, leaving a little space between each biscuit, and bake for 15 minutes, or until golden brown. Remove from the oven and, while still warm, use a round 5 cm (2 in) cookie cutter to cut the biscuits out into neat circles. Transfer to a wire rack and leave to cool completely.

While the biscuits are cooling, make the buttercream. Scoop the avocado flesh into a bowl and mash with a fork. Weigh out 80 g (2¾ oz) of the mashed avocado and beat it together with the butter, cream cheese, vanilla and icing sugar until smooth. Refrigerate until ready for use.

To assemble the sandwiches, spoon half a teaspoon of the buttercream on the underside of a cooled biscuit, top with a sprinkling of crispy kale crumbs and sandwich together with another biscuit. Pop a small amount of buttercream on the top of the sandwich and decorate with a few more kale crumbs and a marigold petal to finish. Repeat with the rest of the biscuits.

—

LIFELESS LEAVES

Harvest your greens by snipping the mature leaves at the stems using scissors. If your freshly picked salad leaves get a little limp once home, reawaken them in a sink of cold water with a few drops of white vinegar. They'll perk up in no time.

A great, quick salad I like to make is chunks of avocado tossed through blanched kale, crispy kale crumbs and marigold petals. It's colourful and full of texture. These cookie sandwiches take the best of the salad's components and send them off on a sugary adventure.

Sweet potato and cumin cakies

Half cake, half cookie, these sweet potato patties deliver a quick burst of cumin that dissolves into a warm, spiced mouthful. Turn them into whoopie pies by filling two cakies with a blend of whipped cream, mashed sweet potato and a sprinkle of icing sugar.

MAKES 16

150 g (5½ oz) sweet potato, peeled and cut into cubes

150 g (5½ oz) soft brown sugar

1 teaspoon vanilla extract

1 teaspoon grated orange zest

1 teaspoon ground coriander

½ teaspoon ground cinnamon

½ teaspoon ground cumin

60 g (2 oz) unsalted butter

1 egg

125 g (4½ oz) plain (all-purpose) flour

2 teaspoons baking powder

35 g (1 oz/½ cup) shredded coconut, toasted

30 g (1 oz) finely grated fresh ginger

3 tablespoons roughly chopped Brazil nuts

SPICE DUST

125 g (4½ oz/1 cup) icing (confectioners') sugar

2 teaspoons ground cumin

Preheat the oven to 200°C (400°F). Line a baking tray with baking paper.

Add the sweet potato pieces to a saucepan of boiling water and cook until tender. Drain, return to the pan and mash until smooth, then set aside to cool.

To make the spice dust, mix the icing sugar and cumin together in a bowl.

Beat the sugar, vanilla, orange zest, coriander, cinnamon, cumin and butter in a bowl using a hand-held mixer, or a stand mixer fitted with the paddle attachment, until fluffy. Add the egg and beat for a further 2 minutes, then fold in the remaining ingredients to form a batter.

Dollop half tablespoonfuls of the batter onto the prepared baking tray and bake for 15 minutes until puffed up and lightly browned around the edges. Remove the cakies from the oven and toss them in the spice dust while still hot. Best served warm.

—

PATIENT PLANTING

Reaping the rewards of your sweet potato plants will take 3–5 months. The plant requires warm sun and good soil, but it's frost-hardy and relatively free from pests and diseases. If you're up for the waiting game, this colourful root crop can keep your pantry full for years.

Apple cider and zucchini muffins

While the inclusion of dates and oats helps bring a breakfast feel to these apple and zucchini muffins, the buzz of cider nudges them over into dessert territory. An energising treat full of texture, these won't last long when they're pulled out of the oven.

MAKES 12

135 g (5 oz/1 cup) grated zucchini (courgette)

240 g (8½ oz/2 cups) grated green apple

160 g (5½ oz/1 cup) finely chopped pitted dates

zest of 1 lemon

250 ml (8½ fl oz/1 cup) apple cider

4 eggs

125 ml (4 fl oz/½ cup) grapeseed oil

110 g (4 oz/½ cup) coconut sugar

2 teaspoons ground cinnamon

2 teaspoons vanilla extract

360 g (9 oz/1¾ cups) plain (all-purpose) flour

200 g (7 oz/2 cups) rolled oats

2 teaspoons baking powder

1 teaspoon salt

Squeeze the grated zucchini and apple to remove any excess moisture, then add them to a bowl together with the dates, lemon zest and cider. Mix everything together well, then leave for 30 minutes to steep.

Preheat the oven to 200°C (400°F). Line a 12-hole standard muffin tin with paper cases.

In a separate bowl, lightly whisk the eggs together with a fork, then add them to the steeped zucchini and apple mixture along with the oil, coconut sugar, cinnamon and vanilla. Stir together well to combine, then slowly fold in the flour, oats, baking powder and salt to form a batter.

Divide the batter among the muffin cases and bake for 30 minutes, or until a skewer inserted into the centres comes out clean. Remove from the oven and leave to cool on a wire rack.

—

ZUCCHINI LOVE

August 8 marks National Zucchini Day, also known as 'Sneak Some Zucchini Onto Your Neighbours' Porch Day' — a magical date when people around the world mysteriously find zucchini outside their front doors. Mark it in your diary.

Chocolate pretzels with jasmine sugar

A twisty treat dusted in springtime sugar. These pretzels are surprisingly easy to make – it takes little effort to roll and shape the dough and you'll be rewarded with delicious chocolate biscuits that you'll be whipping up for years.

MAKES 18

125 g (4½ oz) unsalted butter

125 g (4½ oz) caster (superfine) sugar

1 egg, separated

60 ml (2 fl oz/¼ cup) milk

250 g (9 oz/1⅔ cups) plain (all-purpose) flour

3 tablespoons Dutch (unsweetened) cocoa powder

¼ teaspoon baking powder

½ teaspoon water

JASMINE SUGAR

10 g (¼ oz/½ cup) jasmine petals

110 g (4 oz/½ cup) raw (demerara) sugar

Cream the butter and sugar together in a bowl using a hand-held mixer, or a stand mixer fitted with the paddle attachment, until light and fluffy. Beat in the egg yolk (not the white!) and milk. With cool hands, gently work the flour, cocoa and baking powder into the mixture to form a dough, then divide it in half. Shape the dough halves into balls, cover with plastic wrap and chill in the refrigerator for 1 hour.

While the dough is chilling, make the jasmine sugar. Using your hands, rub the jasmine petals into the sugar in a bowl until the petals are thoroughly mashed (you want to infuse every grain of sugar here with the jasmine flavour, so don't be afraid to be rough).

Preheat the oven to 190°C (375°F). Line a baking tray with baking paper.

Unwrap the refrigerated dough, pull off a marble-sized piece and roll it out into a thin rope on a lightly floured work surface. Lay it out in a semi-circle, then twist the ends up and over each other to make a pretzel shape. Transfer to the prepared baking tray and repeat until you've used up all the dough.

Lightly beat the egg white together with the water to form a glaze. Using a pastry brush, lightly brush the pretzels with the glaze, then sprinkle over the jasmine sugar. Bake for 10–15 minutes until firm. Remove from the oven and leave to cool slightly on the tray for 5 minutes, then transfer to a wire rack and leave to cool completely.

—

SWEET DREAMS

Plant your jasmine near a bedroom window. During the night, the temperature of the jasmine vine will drop, which triggers the opening of the flowers and the strongest release of perfume.

CHOCOLATE PRETZELS WITH JASMINE SUGAR – Page 143

Crispy choc chunk cookies

They're sweet, they're crunchy, they're starchy and chocolatey. There will be no complaints.

MAKES 24

250 g (9 oz) unsalted butter

120 g (4½ oz/1 cup) caster (superfine) sugar

120 g (4½ oz/⅔ cup) soft brown sugar

2 teaspoons vanilla extract

1 teaspoon sea salt

2 eggs

400 g (14 oz/2⅔ cups) plain (all-purpose) flour

1 teaspoon baking powder

250 g (9 oz) good-quality dark or milk chocolate chips

KALE CRISPS

3 kale leaves, tough central stems removed

1 tablespoon extra-virgin olive oil

POTATO CHIPS (CRISPS)

1 potato

1–2 teaspoons melted butter

Preheat the oven to 180°C (350°F). Line three baking trays with baking paper.

For the kale crisps, wash and dry the kale leaves and tear them into small pieces, then transfer to a bowl, drizzle over the oil and mix to coat evenly. Pat the kale pieces with paper towel to remove any excess oil, then spread them out on one of the prepared trays and bake for 15 minutes, or until crispy and brown but not burnt. Remove from the oven and leave to cool, then tear into fine pieces.

Increase the oven temperature to 200°C (400°F).

For the potato chips, thinly slice the potato using a mandoline on its finest setting. Brush the slices lightly with the melted butter and bake on the lined baking tray for 15 minutes, turning halfway through cooking, until golden brown all over. Remove from the oven and leave to cool completely, then break into 2 cm (¾ in) chunks. (To save time you can use store-bought potato chips instead of making your own; just be sure to choose a high-quality thin chip and reduce the salt quantity in this recipe to ¼ teaspoon.)

Cream the butter, sugars, vanilla and salt together in a bowl or in a stand mixer until light and fluffy. Beat in the eggs one by one, then gently mix in the flour and baking powder to form a sticky dough. Stir in the chocolate pieces, then gently fold in the kale crisps and potato chips.

Scoop out golf-ball-sized lumps of the batter, shape them into discs and arrange on the remaining baking tray, leaving around 5 cm (2 in) between each to allow for spreading.

Bake for about 15 minutes, or until golden brown around the edges. Remove from the oven and leave to cool slightly on the tray for 5 minutes, then transfer to a wire rack and leave to cool completely.

—

JUST A PRETTY FACE

While there are plenty of colourful ornamental kale varieties that will help turn your garden into a magical scene fit for an oompa loompa, these flowering kales, though edible, are rather tasteless. For flavour, it's best to stick to the less attractive green, leafy versions instead.

Peanut butter, pretzel and rosemary salt cookies

These cookies are a herby mash-up of everyone's favourite bar snacks; pretzels and peanuts. If only the writers of *Cheers* had had them to hand, they could have written the perfect episode, with Diane Chambers stealing the heart of Sam Malone with one chewy bite.

MAKES 16

- 170 g (6 oz) unsalted butter
- 300 g (10½ oz/1⅓ cups) raw (demerara) sugar
- 100 ml (3½ fl oz) glucose syrup
- 6 teaspoons Rosemary salt (see below)
- 100 g (3½ oz) crunchy peanut butter
- 150 g (5½ oz) ABC butter (almond, Brazil nut and cashew nut butter)
- 2 eggs
- 2 teaspoons vanilla extract
- 225 g (8 oz/1½ cups) plain (all-purpose) flour
- 1 teaspoon baking powder
- 40 g (1½ oz/¼ cup) roughly chopped raw peanuts
- 16 pretzel crisps

ROSEMARY SALT

- 3 rosemary sprigs, leaves removed
- 160 g (5½ oz/½ cup) rock salt

PRETZEL CRUNCH

- 110 g (4 oz) unsalted butter
- 40 g (1½ oz) caster (superfine) sugar
- 20 g (¾ oz) soft brown sugar
- 170 g (6 oz) plain (all-purpose) flour
- 100 g (3½ oz) pretzel crisps, crushed into pea-sized pieces

To make the rosemary salt, blitz the rosemary leaves and rock salt in a food processor or spice grinder until fine. Pass through a sieve and set aside.

For the pretzel crunch, cream the butter and sugars together in a bowl using a hand-held mixer, or a stand mixer fitted with the paddle attachment, until light and fluffy. Gently fold in the flour, then the pretzel pieces. On a lightly floured surface roll the mixture into a ball and cover with plastic wrap, then chill in the refrigerator for 30 minutes.

Preheat the oven to 190°C (375°F). Line a baking tray with greased baking paper.

Once chilled, break the pretzel crunch mixture up into small pieces, arrange them on the prepared baking tray in an even layer and bake for 20 minutes, or until lightly golden. Leave to cool completely.

While the pretzel crunch is cooking, make the cookies by beating together the butter, sugar, glucose and 4 teaspoons of the rosemary salt in a bowl or in a stand mixer until fluffy, at least 10 minutes. Add the nut butters, eggs and vanilla and beat for a further 6 minutes until smooth and voluminous, then gently mix in the flour, baking powder, peanuts and 2 teaspoons of the rosemary salt. Stir through 250 g (9 oz) of the baked pretzel crunch, then cover the cookie dough with plastic wrap and refrigerate for at least 1 hour.

When ready to bake, scoop out tablespoons of the chilled dough and dollop them onto a lined baking tray, leaving around 5 cm (2 in) between them to allow for spreading. Push a whole pretzel into the top of each dough mound and dust generously with rosemary salt, then bake for 20 minutes or until golden. Remove from the oven and leave to cool slightly on the tray for 5 minutes, then transfer to a wire rack and leave to cool completely.

—

MIST OF THE SEA

Rosemary's name originates from the Latin *rosmarinus*, meaning 'mist of the sea', and this drought-resistant herb grows wild along the sea cliffs of Italy, Greece, Spain and France. Mimic these conditions by positioning your rosemary in full sun and in well-drained, sandy soil.

Persian love logs

Year after year my Persian love cake is one of my biggest sellers, the exotic punch of rose and cardamom blanketed in creamy Greek yoghurt making it an irresistible bite. This recipe sees the best of this cake transformed into one of the simplest biscuits you can make. Keep it up your sleeve for last-minute guests.

MAKES 24

155 g (5½ oz/1½ cups) ground almonds

225 g (8 oz/1½ cups) plain (all-purpose) flour

230 g (8 oz/1 cup) caster (superfine) sugar

230 g (8 oz/1 cup) dark brown sugar

½ teaspoon salt

115 g (4 oz) unsalted butter, softened

2 large eggs

3 tablespoons rosewater

1 teaspoon ground cardamom

35 g (1¼ oz/¼ cup) pistachio kernels, finely chopped

5 g (¼ oz/¼ cup) dried rose petals

Preheat the oven to 175°C (345°F). Line a baking tray with baking paper.

Using your fingertips, mix the ground almonds, flour, sugars, salt and softened butter together in a bowl to form a clumpy, loose dough. Using a wooden spoon, mix in the eggs one at a time followed by the rosewater and cardamom.

Divide the sticky dough into 24 equal-sized pieces, shape into logs and place on the prepared baking tray. Gently press the pistachio kernels and rose petals into the top of the logs and bake for 45 minutes until firm. Remove from the oven and leave to cool slightly on the tray for 5 minutes, then transfer to a wire rack and leave to cool completely.

—

A NUMBERS GAME

Rambling and climbing roses are less rigid than typical rose bushes, making them a pretty yet versatile bloom. What's the difference between a rambler and a climber? Ramblers have flexible stems to help coax them to climb over fences and surfaces and mostly flower just once a year in clusters of seven, while climbers are a little tougher in the skin department and will bloom repeatedly but only in clusters of five.

Miso eggplant brownies

I love *nasu dengaku* – the Japanese side-dish of tender eggplants glazed in miso, mirin and sake. The more I eat it, the more I want those flavours in a brownie. So here it is. The miso brings a beautiful umami to the brownie's chewy outer while the eggplants add to the silken fudge centre. It's quite possibly the best brownie you'll eat.

MAKES 8

6 long thin eggplants (aubergines)

2 tablespoons vegetable oil

65 g (2¼ oz/¼ cup) white miso paste

4 teaspoons honey, plus extra to taste

4 teaspoons mirin

95 g (3¼ oz/½ cup) soft brown sugar, plus extra for sprinkling

150 g (5½ oz/1 cup) plain (all-purpose) flour

1 teaspoon baking powder

30 g (1 oz/¼ cup) Dutch (unsweetened) cocoa powder

4 eggs

200 g (7 oz) unsalted butter

200 g (7 oz) good-quality dark chocolate (approx. 60% cocoa solids), broken into chunks

230 g (8 oz/1 cup) caster (superfine) sugar

Preheat the oven to 170°C (340°F). Grease and line a 30 × 20 cm (12 × 8 in) brownie tin with baking paper.

Halve the eggplants lengthways and score the flesh with a sharp knife in a deep criss-cross pattern. Soak the eggplant halves in cold salted water for 15 minutes to remove any bitterness, then drain and pat dry. Generously brush the cut sides with the oil and place, skin side down, on a baking tray. Bake for 40 minutes, or until browned.

Stir 4 teaspoons of the miso together with the honey and mirin to form a paste. Spread the paste in an even layer over the cut sides of the eggplant halves and top with a sprinkle of soft brown sugar, then return to the oven for 5–10 minutes, or until caramelised at the edges. Remove from the oven and leave to cool completely before scooping out and reserving the flesh, discarding any seeds.

Reduce the oven temperature to 160°C (320°F).

Whisk the flour, baking powder and cocoa powder together in a bowl and set aside. In a separate bowl, lightly whisk the eggs together with the remainder of the miso until smooth. Set aside.

Gently melt the butter and chocolate in a heatproof bowl set over a saucepan of lightly simmering water, stirring until completely smooth. Remove from the heat and leave to cool slightly, then stir in the sugars. Gradually stir in the egg and miso mixture, then fold in the dry ingredients to form a batter. Swirl in 90 g (3 oz/⅓ cup) of the eggplant flesh, then pour the brownie batter into the prepared tin and bake for 30 minutes (this will give you a nice, gooey centre). Remove from the oven and leave to cool in the tin before cutting into pieces.

—

BITTER GOODBYES

Pick eggplants while they're young and shiny for the best taste – the bigger eggplants are less enjoyable because they're spongier, more bitter and have chunkier seed sections. Pay attention to the skin too; the thicker the skin, the less tender the flesh.

Herbed salted honey bars

These bars salute the pure wild beauty of honey. Woody herbs like thyme, sage and rosemary work really well in this mix, but feel free to bend the recipe to suit your taste buds by switching them out for the herb you like best. Ditto the nuts.

MAKES 12

125 ml (4 fl oz/½ cup) honey

15 g (½ oz/¼ cup) chopped fresh herbs (such as thyme, sage or rosemary)

460 g (1 lb/2 cups) caster (superfine) sugar

375 ml (12½ fl oz/1½ cup) grapeseed oil

2 large eggs

600 g (1 lb 5 oz/4 cups) plain (all-purpose) flour

2 teaspoons bicarbonate of soda (baking soda)

1 teaspoon sea salt flakes, plus extra for garnish

135 g (5 oz/1 cup) chopped macadamia nuts

Preheat the oven to 175°C (345°F). Line a 30 × 20 cm (12 × 8 in) baking tin with baking paper.

Stir the honey and herbs together in a bowl, Add the sugar, oil and eggs and beat together until frothy and well combined. Gradually whisk in the flour, bicarbonate of soda and salt, then stir through the macadamia nuts to incorporate evenly.

Spoon the mixture into the prepared baking tin and spread it out in an even layer with a palette knife, then bake for 30 minutes, or until golden brown.

Remove from the oven and leave to cool slightly in the tin before transferring to a wire rack. Cut into bars and sprinkle a little extra sea salt over each before serving.

—

BEE BREAD

With its hairy, upside-down flowers that bees love to swing from, borage is an important honey plant; its unrivalled ability to attract these pollinators has led to it being given the nickname 'bee bread'. It's also incredibly easy to grow in well-drained soil. Pop some in your plot this weekend.

Carrot and grapefruit curd tarts

These guys look like a lemon tart with a Florida suntan. The deep shade of gold is thanks to the yin-yang balance of bitter grapefruit and sweet carrots. The creamy components of the curd smooth out the acidity here, while the snap of the ginger crust shakes it all back together again.

MAKES 10

½ pink grapefruit

6 carrots

450 g (1 lb/2 cups) caster (superfine) sugar

4 teaspoons cornflour (cornstarch)

zest of 1 orange

4 egg yolks

4 eggs

175 g (6 oz) unsalted butter, chilled and cut into cubes

GINGER CRUST

1 × quantity Garden jam drop biscuits (page 128)

1 teaspoon ground ginger

4 teaspoons milk powder

80–100 g (2¾–3½ oz) unsalted butter, melted

Pass the grapefruit and carrots through a juicer and measure out 250 ml (8½ fl oz/1 cup) of the combined juice. Whisk the sugar, cornflour and orange zest together in a high-sided saucepan, then whisk in the grapefruit and carrot juice. Whisk in the egg yolks one by one followed by the whole eggs.

Over a low heat whisk in the chilled butter, then increase the heat to medium–high and cook, whisking continuously, for 10 minutes or until the curd has thickened and is bubbling away nicely. Turn the heat off and whisk vigorously, then pour into a stainless steel bowl and cover with plastic wrap. Chill for 2 hours to firm.

Lightly grease ten 6 cm (2½ in) fluted tart tins or mini aluminium pie tins.

While the curd is chilling, make the crust. Add the biscuits to a food processor and pulse to a rough crumb, then transfer to a bowl and stir together with the ginger and milk powder to combine. Add the melted butter 1 tablespoon at a time until a rough dough forms (you don't want it too sticky and buttery, you just need it to hold its shape against your tart tins). Once you have the right consistency, press the cookie dough into the base and sides of your prepared tins, then chill in the refrigerator for 1 hour.

Preheat the oven to 175°C (345°F).

Spoon the chilled curd into the cooled tart tins and spread it out to fill evenly, then transfer the tins to the oven and bake for 5–10 minutes until the filling has set. Remove from the oven and leave to cool slightly in the tins for 5 minutes, then transfer to a wire rack to cool completely.

Strawberry and elderflower muffins

Brimming with berries, these muffins make me think of an English summer party: light, girly and a little bit swish.

MAKES 12

250 g (9 oz) unsalted butter

1 teaspoon vanilla extract

170 g (6 oz/¾ cup) caster (superfine) sugar

3 eggs

25 ml (¾ fl oz) milk

300 g (10½ oz/2 cups) plain (all-purpose) flour

1 teaspoon baking powder

pinch of salt

1 teaspoon freshly ground black pepper

150 g (5½ oz/1 cup) fresh strawberries, hulled and quartered

ELDERFLOWER SYRUP

40 g (1½ oz/2 cups) elderflower heads

salt

220 g (8 oz/1 cup) sugar

375 ml (12½ fl oz/1½ cups) water

STREUSEL

300 g (10½ oz/2 cups) plain (all-purpose) flour

350 g (12½ oz) raw (demerara) sugar

220 g (8 oz) unsalted butter

Preheat the oven to 175°C (345°F). Line a 12-hole standard muffin tin with paper cases.

To make the syrup, wash the elderflower heads thoroughly in cold, salted water, then pluck the blossoms off the stems and rinse. Transfer the blossoms to a saucepan with the sugar and water and bring to a gentle boil. Reduce the heat to low and leave to simmer for 10 minutes, then remove from the heat and set aside to steep.

Meanwhile, melt half the butter in a saucepan over a low heat until frothy and nicely browned. Strain through a fine-mesh sieve into a mixing bowl, add the vanilla, sugar and the rest of the butter and beat together until light and fluffy.

Beat the eggs into the mixture one by one, then gently fold in the milk, 185 ml (6 fl oz/¾ cup) of the elderflower syrup and the flour, baking powder, salt and pepper. Continuing to fold gently, drop the strawberry pieces into the batter in small handfuls until evenly distributed.

To make the streusel, rub all the ingredients together in a bowl with your fingertips to form a crumble-like mixture.

Spoon the batter evenly into the paper cases, press a small amount of the streusel mixture into the top of each and bake for 45 minutes, or until a skewer inserted into the centre of a muffin comes out clean. Remove from the oven and pour over the remainder of the syrup while the muffins are in the tin and still warm.

—

RIPE FOR THE PICKING

Elderflower bushes are frost-hardy and very easy to grow from cuttings. Wear gloves when you're pinching an overhanging branch from your neighbour's garden as the leaves, branches and roots can be toxic if ingested (come time for harvesting remember to pick the blossoms with care too). An elderflower bush can grow up to 3 m (9 ft 10 in) high and, apart from the edible blossoms, will reward you with small edible cooking berries with a flavour similar to blackberries.

Lilac and blackberry cheesecakes

Lilac's citrus notes fit cosily inside these tangy baked cheesecakes. Blackberries add a sour, brambly flavour while the chocolate crust helps keeps things earthy.

MAKES 8

200 g (7 oz) cream cheese

10 g (¼ oz/½ cup) lilac petals, washed and stamens removed

55 g (2 oz/¼ cup) caster (superfine) sugar

1 teaspoon vanilla extract

pinch of salt

2 eggs

200 g (7 oz) sour cream

3 teaspoons plain (all-purpose) flour

130 g (4½ oz/1 cup) blackberries

COCOA CRUST

125 g (4½ oz) unsalted butter

125 g (4½ oz) caster (superfine) sugar

1 egg yolk

60 ml (2 fl oz/¼ cup) milk

250 g (9 oz/1⅓ cups) plain (all-purpose) flour

3 tablespoons Dutch (unsweetened) cocoa powder

¼ teaspoon baking powder

½ teaspoon water

To make the cocoa crust, cream the butter and sugar together in a bowl using a hand-held mixer, or a stand mixer fitted with the paddle attachment, until light and fluffy. Beat in the egg yolk and milk. With cool hands, gently work the flour, cocoa, baking powder and water into the mixture to form a dough, then divide it in half. Shape the dough halves into balls, cover with plastic wrap and chill in the refrigerator for 1 hour.

Preheat the oven to 200°C (400°F). Lightly grease eight 10 cm (4 in) individual foil pie tins.

Once chilled, drop a heaped tablespoon of the cookie dough into the centre of each pie tin. Using damp fingertips, push the dough down evenly into the base and sides of the tin.

Beat the cream cheese, lilac petals, sugar, vanilla and salt together in a bowl using a hand-held blender, or a stand mixer fitted with the paddle attachment, on high speed until fully incorporated. On a low speed, beat in the eggs one by one, then add the sour cream and flour and beat until smooth.

Pour the filling into your crusts and push four blackberries into the filling for each cheesecake. Arrange the tins on a baking tray and bake for 10 minutes, or until the centre of the cream cheese filling is set. Leave to cool completely before serving.

—

POT LUCK

Lilac bushes love their own nook in the garden and come in several colour shades, all of which are great for luring butterflies. Plant them from seedlings into well-drained pots with light shade. Prune the woody branches often to keep the blossoms full.

Galletas de jardín
(Mexican garden cookies)

These little delights are a play on the Mexican wedding cookies, *pastitas de boda*. Marigolds and pineapple sage inject a fruity, Central American edge into these heavily romantic sweets. My hunch is you'll want to double the batch.

MAKES 20

225 g (8 oz) unsalted butter

280 g (10 oz/2¼ cups) icing (confectioners') sugar, sifted

½ teaspoon ground cinnamon

1 teaspoon vanilla extract

½ teaspoon almond extract

100 g (3½ oz/1 cup) ground almonds

300 g (10½ oz/2 cups) plain (all-purpose) flour

¼ teaspoon salt

155 g (5½ oz/⅓ cup) whole almonds, roughly chopped

5 g (¼ oz/¼ cup) marigold petals, plus extra to decorate

5 g (¼ oz/¼ cup) pineapple sage petals, plus extra to decorate

pinch of chilli powder, to taste

Preheat the oven to 175°C (345°F). Line a baking tray with baking paper.

Cream the butter and 125 g (4½ oz) of the icing sugar together in a bowl using a hand-held mixer, or a stand mixer fitted with the paddle attachment, until light and fluffy. Beat in the cinnamon, vanilla and almond extracts, ground almonds, flour and salt until a soft dough forms, then gently fold in the chopped almonds and flower petals.

Roll the dough out into balls about 3 cm (1¼ in) in diameter and place them on the prepared baking tray, leaving around 2 cm (¾ in) between each. Bake for 15 minutes until firm.

Meanwhile, place the remaining icing sugar in a bowl.

Remove the cookies from the oven and leave to cool slightly on the tray, then toss generously in the icing sugar while still warm. Return the cookies to the tray and leave them to cool completely, then toss them once more in the icing sugar. Sprinkle with chilli powder to taste along with a few extra flower petals to decorate.

—

RAINBOW BRIGHT

Pineapple sage is an edible native to Mexico, so it makes sense that it loves the sun. Its bright green leaves and vivid red trumpet flowers can be grown outdoors and indoors. If growing indoors, keep it in a nook that stays warm when the temperature drops overnight and, while you're awake and checking up on your plant, use the petals to brew yourself a cup of tangy tea.

Sunflower biscotti

An Italian gem, brightened up with rays of yellow petals and a hippy crunch of sunflower kernels.

MAKES 20

310 g (10½ oz/2½ cups)
  plain (all-purpose) flour

1 teaspoon baking powder

1 teaspoon bicarbonate of
  soda (baking soda)

150 g (5½ oz) caster
  (superfine) sugar

5 g (¼ oz/¼ cup) sunflower
  petals, roughly torn

3 eggs, lightly beaten

1 teaspoon vanilla extract

zest of 3 oranges

150 g (5½ oz/1¼ cups)
  sunflower kernels,
  toasted

200 g (5½ oz/2 cups)
  walnuts, toasted and
  roughly chopped

Preheat the oven to 170°C (340°F). Line a baking tray with baking paper.

Whisk the flour, baking powder, bicarbonate of soda, sugar and sunflower petals together. Gently whisk in the eggs, vanilla and orange zest to form a soft dough. Add the sunflower kernels and walnut pieces and turn out onto a floured surface. Knead lightly to a firm dough.

Divide the dough into three equal-sized pieces and roll each into a log about 10 cm (4 in) in diameter. Flatten the top of each log a little to make a classic biscotti shape.

Transfer the logs to the prepared baking tray and bake for 30 minutes until golden. Remove from the oven and leave to cool slightly for 5 minutes on the tray, then transfer to a wire rack and leave to cool completely.

Reduce the oven temperature to 150°C (300°F).

Using a sharp knife, cut the logs diagonally into pieces roughly 1 cm (½ in) thick, as if you were cutting a loaf of bread. Place each biscotti piece, cut-side down, on the baking tray and bake for another 10–15 minutes, or until dried out and crunchy. Leave to cool completely before serving.

—

SUN BAKING FOR SURVIVAL

Sunflowers are one of a small handful of plant species that turn to face the sun. Known as heliotropism, sunflowers track light to warm themselves, which in turn attracts bees and other pollinators. Give your sunflowers a helping hand by planting them in a spot that receives at least 6 hours of sunlight per day.

Avocado and pea cookies

The wholesome, fatty beats of avocados and coconut oil mingle with the green, true notes of peas to create a beauty of a treat. Colourful and pillowy, they're sure to be the most popular kid in your cookie jar.

MAKES 20

40 g (1½ oz) peas, fresh or frozen

2 ripe avocados

80 g (2½ oz/⅓ cup) coconut oil, chilled until solid

2 teaspoons vanilla extract

165 g (6 oz/¾ cup) sugar

2 eggs

300 g (10½ oz/2 cups) plain (all-purpose) flour

2 teaspoons bicarbonate of soda (baking soda)

¼ teaspoon salt

130 g (4½ oz/¾ cup) white chocolate chips

Preheat the oven to 175°C (345°F). Line a baking tray with baking paper.

Add the peas to a saucepan of boiling water and cook until tender. Drain and leave to cool slightly, then transfer to a bowl and blitz with a hand-held blender to form a purée.

Slice the avocados in half lengthways, remove the stones and scoop the flesh into a bowl. Using a hand-held blender, blitz to a purée, then add the coconut oil, vanilla and sugar and beat until smooth. Beat in the eggs one by one followed by the pea purée, then fold in the remaining ingredients to form a uniform, bright green batter.

Scoop out tablespoons of the batter and dollop them onto the prepared baking tray. Bake for 30 minutes, or until lightly browned on the underside. Remove from the oven and leave to cool slightly on the tray for 5 minutes, then transfer to a wire rack and leave to cool completely.

—

ALLIGATOR PEAR

This is an old colloquialism for avocados. Practise dropping the term while you propagate your avocado tree from seed. You'll need to wait 4-6 years for your alligator pears to appear. Plenty of time to get the term in circulation again.

Beetella fudge fingers

Meet 'beetella' – a mature Nutella with a peek of beetroot. The perfect home for this chocolate spread is sandwiched between two crumbly cocoa biscuits and perched beside an espresso martini. Any excess is also great spread over ricotta French toast or stuffed inside a rugelach (page 137).

MAKES 12

250 g (9 oz/1⅔ cups) plain (all-purpose) flour

30 g (1 oz/¼ cup) Dutch (unsweetened) cocoa powder

100 g (3½ oz) icing (confectioners') sugar

200 g (7 oz) unsalted butter, chilled and cut into cubes

2 egg yolks

1 teaspoon vanilla extract

BEETELLA

300 g (10½ oz) beetroot (beets), peeled and cut into chunks

200 g (7 oz/2 cups) nut butter (almond, cashew or Brazil)

185 g (6½ oz/1½ cups) Dutch (unsweetened) cocoa powder

1 teaspoon vanilla extract

125 g (4½ oz/1 cup) icing (confectioners') sugar

60 ml (2 fl oz/¼ cup) thick (double/heavy) cream

For the beetella, steam the beetroot until tender, then leave to cool. Transfer to a food processor or blender together with the remaining ingredients and blitz until smooth. Refrigerate until needed.

Combine the flour, cocoa and icing sugar together in a bowl and rub through the chilled butter to form fine crumbs. Stir in the egg yolks and vanilla to form a soft dough, then turn it out onto a floured surface. Gently shape the dough into a rectangular slab approximately 2 cm (¾ in) thick. Cover with plastic wrap and refrigerate for 30 minutes.

Preheat the oven to 200°C (400°F). Line a baking tray with baking paper.

Once chilled, roll out the dough to a 1 cm (½ in) thickness and cut it into 24 fingers approximately 4 cm (1½ in) wide. Place on the prepared tray, leaving around 2 cm (¾ in) between each finger, and bake for 10 minutes, or until firm to the touch. Remove from the oven and leave to cool slightly for 5 minutes on the tray, then transfer to a wire rack and leave to cool completely.

To assemble, generously slather a biscuit finger with the beetella, then sandwich together with another biscuit finger. Repeat with the rest of the biscuits and beetella.

—

SHADY LADIES

Beetroot can grow in partially sunny positions, so they're a good vegetable to try growing if you aren't blessed with a spot in full sun. Prior to planting, soak the seeds in water overnight to help with germination. Other shade-loving edibles include lettuces, radishes and nasturtium.

Peppermint and geranium cheesecake slice

A crunchy after-dinner mint with a hint of garden freshness. Serve frozen for a refreshing iced dessert or at room temperature with a sprinkling of icing sugar.

MAKES 8

680 g (1½ lb) cream cheese

180 g (6½ oz) caster (superfine) sugar

80 g (2¾ oz) sour cream

4 eggs

35 g (1¼ oz/¼ cup) plain (all-purpose) flour

1 teaspoon peppermint essence

1 teaspoon vanilla extract

2–3 drops of natural green food dye (optional)

BASE

500 g (1 lb 2 oz) dark chocolate biscuits (such as Beetella fudge fingers, see facing page)

3 teaspoons very finely diced peppermint geranium leaves

1 teaspoon salt

160 g (5½ oz/1¼ cups) Dutch (unsweetened) cocoa powder

240 g (8½ oz) unsalted butter, melted

Line a 30 × 20 cm (12 × 8 in) baking tin with baking paper.

For the base, put the biscuits in a bowl and crush to a fine crumb with the end of a rolling pin. Stir in the geranium leaves, salt and cocoa, then add the melted butter slowly, stirring, to form a rough dough (you should be able to form it into solid clumps without it crumbling). Press the dough mixture evenly over the base of the prepared tin, cover with plastic wrap and refrigerate for 1 hour or until set.

Preheat the oven to 180°C (350°F).

Beat the cream cheese, caster sugar and sour cream together in a bowl using a hand-held mixer, or a stand mixer fitted with the paddle attachment, until smooth. Add the eggs one at a time followed by the flour, peppermint essence, vanilla and food dye (if using, to give the filling a vibrant minty tone).

Remove the set biscuit base from the refrigerator, take off the plastic wrap and spread the filling over it evenly. Bake for 30 minutes or until the filling is set and lightly brown around the edges. Remove from the oven and leave to cool in the tin. Cut into long thin slices to serve.

—

A FRESH SPLASH

Make your own peppermint essence by steeping 40 g (1½ oz/1 cup) fresh peppermint leaves with 250 ml (8½ fl oz/1 cup) vodka in a sterilised jar, bruising and bashing the leaves to release the peppermint oil before covering them with the spirit. Seal the jar and let the brew sit for 3–4 weeks before use.

Molasses and rocket flower gingerbread

These deeply spiced cookies are given an extra peppery kick from the rocket leaves and flowers. Delicious with or without the dark chocolate glaze. Fun to make, fun to eat.

MAKES 16

100 g (3½ oz) unsalted butter, chilled and cut into cubes

175 g (6 oz/¾ cup) soft brown sugar

300 g (10½ oz/2 cups) plain (all-purpose) flour

2 teaspoons baking powder

¼ teaspoon sea salt

2 teaspoons ground ginger

½ teaspoon ground cinnamon

½ teaspoon ground allspice

½ teaspoon freshly grated nutmeg

1 egg, lightly beaten

115 g (4 oz/⅓ cup) molasses

3 tablespoons finely chopped rocket (arugula)

3 tablespoons rocket flower petals, plus extra to garnish

CHOCOLATE GLAZE

450 g (1 lb) good-quality dark chocolate (approx. 60% cocoa solids), broken into chunks

1 tablespoon vegetable oil

Preheat the oven to 190°C (375°F). Line a baking tray with baking paper.

Using your hands, rub the butter and sugar together with the dry ingredients in a bowl to form coarse breadcrumbs. Stir in the egg and molasses with a spoon to form a soft dough, then add the rocket and flower petals and combine.

Divide the mixture into three equal-sized pieces, turn each out onto a lightly flowered surface and knead lightly. Take one piece and roll it out to a 5 mm (¼ in) thickness, then punch out cookies using your favourite cutter. Repeat with the remaining dough.

Place the cookies on the prepared baking tray and bake for 10 minutes, or until firm around the edges. Remove from the oven and leave to cool slightly on the tray for 5 minutes, then transfer to a wire rack and leave to cool completely.

While the cookies are cooling, make the chocolate glaze. Place the chocolate and oil in a heatproof bowl set over a saucepan of lightly simmering water and heat gently, stirring, until the chocolate has melted and the mixture is completely smooth.

Remove the bowl from the heat and dip one side of each cooled cookie in the chocolate glaze. Scatter a few extra rocket flower petals over the chocolate to decorate.

—

MORPH CODE

Rocket leaves change shape as the plant matures. From seedlings, the leaves are soft and oval. They'll continue to grow into their most supple, edible shape, which resembles a feather silhouette. And finally, as the plant gets older and shoots up flowers to reseed, the leaves become thinner and tougher and are at their least enjoyable to chew.

MOLASSES AND ROCKET FLOWER GINGERBREAD – Page 168

Coconut and coriander cream pie

This beauty is the kind of cream pie destined to be thrown in someone's face ... lovingly, of course. But if you're gonna make a slapstick pie, it better taste good. This one's packed with a deep, rich coconut custard and the gentle jungle scent of coriander. If you can, shred the flesh from a real hairy coconut for maximum flavour and authenticity.

SERVES 10–12

1 teaspoon ground coriander

560 ml (19 fl oz/2¼ cups) coconut milk

145 g (5 oz/⅔ cup) caster (superfine) sugar

1 teaspoon vanilla extract

4 large egg yolks

35 g (1¼ oz/¼ cup) plain (all-purpose) flour

3 tablespoons cornflour (cornstarch)

pinch of salt

45 g (1½ oz/¾ cup) shredded coconut, toasted

3 tablespoons unsalted butter

500 ml (17 fl oz/2 cups) whipping cream

3 tablespoons finely chopped coriander (cilantro) leaves

COCONUT CRUST

185 g (6½ oz/1¼ cups) plain (all-purpose) flour

45 g (1½ oz/¼ cup) coconut flour

2 teaspoons caster (superfine) sugar

½ teaspoon salt

125 g (4½ oz) unsalted butter, chilled and cut into cubes

60 ml (2 fl oz/¼ cup) cold water

To make the crust, stir together the flours, sugar and salt in a bowl to combine. Using your fingers, rub in the chilled butter to form a rough dough, then add the water 1 tablespoon at a time, mixing everything together with a butter knife until smooth. Shape the dough into a flat disc, cover in plastic wrap and chill for 30 minutes.

Preheat the oven to 180°C (350°F). Lightly grease and line a 22 cm (9 in) round pie tin with baking paper.

Once chilled, roll out the dough to a 5 mm (¼ in) thickness and use it to line the base and sides of the prepared pie tin. Cover with baking paper, weigh down with baking beads or uncooked rice and bake blind for 10 minutes. Remove from the oven and leave to cool.

While the pastry crust is cooling, make the filling. Add the ground coriander and coconut milk to a heavy-based saucepan and bring to the boil, then remove from the heat, cover with a lid and set aside to infuse.

Beat the sugar, vanilla and egg yolks together in a large bowl until very thick and yellow, about 10 minutes. Add the flour, cornflour and salt and stir together well. Still stirring, pour over the warm coconut milk to combine, then pour the mixture into the saucepan and cook over a medium heat for a few minutes more until the custard has thickened up enough to coat the back of a wooden spoon. Stir in half the shredded coconut and the butter until melted, then pour into a bowl, cover with plastic wrap and chill in the refrigerator for 2 hours.

In a bowl, whip the cream to soft peaks.

Once chilled, pour the custard filling into the cooled pastry shell and top with the whipped cream, the remainder of the shredded coconut and the chopped coriander leaves.

WANNABE CARROT

Confetti coriander is a delicate heirloom herb with a sweeter taste than regular coriander and feathery leaves that resemble carrot tops. It grows faster and takes longer to mature to seed too, so you'll have longer to cook with it.

Elderflower and cashew blondies

When you've hit your brownie limit, take a breath and then turn to a blondie instead. Less rich but just as comforting, a blondie offers up the same gooey luxury but at the other end of the chocolate spectrum. You can substitute the elderflower in this recipe for any other delicate flower. Jasmine, chamomile or honeysuckle all work well.

MAKES 12

5 elderflower heads

salt

225 g (8 oz) unsalted butter

350 g (12½ oz/2 cups) white chocolate chips

95 g (3¼ oz/½ cup) soft brown sugar

300 g (10½ oz/2 cups) plain (all-purpose) flour

2 teaspoons baking powder

½ teaspoon salt

3 tablespoons milk powder

4 eggs

1 teaspoon vanilla extract

155 g (5½ oz/1 cup) cashews, roughly chopped

Preheat the oven to 175°C (345°F). Grease and line a 30 × 20 cm (12 × 8 in) brownie tin with baking paper.

Wash the elderflower heads thoroughly in cold, salted water, then pluck the blossoms off the stems and rinse. Transfer the blossoms to a bowl, or a stand mixer fitted with the paddle attachment, and beat together with the butter until light and fluffy, about 10 minutes.

Add the butter and elderflower mixture to a small heavy-based saucepan and melt gently over a low heat, then strain into a heatproof bowl, discarding the elderflower blossoms. Add the chocolate to the bowl, set it over a saucepan of lightly simmering water and melt gently, stirring, until completely smooth. Stir in the sugar, remove from the heat and leave to cool slightly.

Once cool, add the flour, baking powder, salt and milk powder to the chocolate mixture and whisk everything together well to combine. Add the eggs and vanilla and whisk again, then fold through the cashews to incorporate evenly.

Pour the blondie batter into the prepared brownie tin and bake for 25–30 minutes, or until a skewer inserted into the centre comes out almost clean with a few moist crumbs attached. Remove from the oven and leave to cool in the tin before cutting into pieces.

—

BEST BUDS

When picking edible flowers, stick to the upper tips for the newest buds. They're sweeter and purer in taste than the bottom rungs. And don't forget to leave some flowers for the bees, to keep your plants pollinated and the world turning.

Apple and fennel galettes

MAKES 4

6 cooking apples

1 fennel bulb, halved, stems removed and fronds reserved for pastry (see below)

3 tablespoons raw (demerara) sugar, plus extra for sprinkling

zest of 1 lemon

½ teaspoon ground cardamom

1 teaspoon freshly grated nutmeg

4 teaspoons ground almonds, plus extra for sprinkling

1 egg

1 tablespoon water

4 teaspoons fennel seeds

40 g (1½ oz) unsalted butter, chilled

FENNEL FROND PASTRY

4 teaspoons finely chopped fennel fronds

375 g (13 oz/2½ cups) plain (all-purpose) flour

75 g (2¾ oz/½ cup) spelt flour

2 tablespoons caster (superfine) sugar

1 teaspoon salt

310 g (11 oz) unsalted butter, chilled and cut into cubes

80 ml (2½ fl oz/⅓ cup) ice-cold water, plus extra if necessary

To make the pastry, mix the fennel fronds, flours, sugar and salt together in a bowl. Using your fingertips add the chilled butter and rub it through the dry ingredients to form a rough dough, then add the cold water and gently mix everything together. Turn the dough out onto a lightly floured surface (being careful, as the dough will be very crumbly), divide it into two equal-sized portions and knead each gently to bring the dough together a little more. Roll the dough portions into balls, cover in plastic wrap and chill in the refrigerator for 1 hour.

While the dough is chilling, make the filling. Peel and core the apples and cut them into roughly 3 mm (⅛ in) thick slices with a mandoline or a very sharp knife, then cut the slices into semi circles. Thinly slice the fennel bulb halves lengthways as per the apple, then trim the pieces into the same shape as the apple slices. Toss the apple and fennel slices together with the sugar, lemon zest, cardamom, nutmeg and ground almonds in a bowl to coat evenly.

Preheat the oven to 180°C (350°F). Line a baking tray with baking paper.

Once chilled, divide the pastry balls in half to leave you with four pieces in total. Place a pastry portion on a floured work surface and knead gently to bring the dough together, adding a little splash of chilled water as you go if you need it to help it bind, then roll out into approximately 5 mm (¼ in) thick rectangles or circles. Sprinkle an extra ½ teaspoon or so of ground almonds and raw sugar over the dough, then arrange the apple and fennel slices in an even layer on top in a pattern of your choice. Fold the edges of the galette up to the outer edges of the slices to form a rough border. Repeat with the remaining dough pieces and apple and fennel slices, then place them on the prepared baking tray.

Whisk the egg and water together to form a wash, then use it to brush the pastry edges. Sprinkle over the fennel seeds and an extra 1 tablespoon or so of raw sugar, dot with the butter and bake for 40 minutes, until golden brown around the edges. Remove from the oven and leave to cool slightly on the tray, then transfer to a wire rack to cool completely.

Fennel brings a lightly perfumed fragrance to the tart cooking apples used in these rustic, wholesome galettes, with both ingredients being tossed in cardamom, nutmeg and lemon zest to help marry them. The galette dough is crumbly and nutty thanks to the addition of spelt flour, and the fennel fronds add veins of green throughout. I love how generous and slightly wobbly they look. Serve with ice cream, please.

Heartfelt thanks to everyone who has supported this project from beginning to end: Natasha Grogan of The Sage Garden, Timothy Hillier, Ellen Spooner, Jane Willson, Loran McDougall, Mark Campbell, Jessica Lowe, Lindsay Harris, Brigid Wald, Tara Pearce, Lauren Taylor, Simon Davis, Kate Hill, Anna Forsyth, Kaz Morton, Sarah Schembri, Azalea Flowers and Georgie's Harvest. Extra appreciation to my round-the-clock believer Rick, baba the taste testing babysitter, my wordsmith brother, food guru mumma, bookworm dad and my perfect lucky charm Ray Lou.

Dedicated to my everythings, R and R.

Hayley McKee is a self-taught baker and owner of Sticky Fingers Bakery, a made-to-order cake business known for inventive cake flavours made with vegetables, homegrown herbs, edible flowers and Australian native ingredients.

Her baked creations and recipes have been commissioned by the likes of *Good Food*, *frankie* magazine, ABC Radio, Warner Brothers Music, The Australian Ballet and fashion house Romance Was Born.

Published in 2018 by Hardie Grant Books, an imprint
of Hardie Grant Publishing

Hardie Grant Books (Melbourne)
Building 1, 658 Church Street
Richmond, Victoria 3121

Hardie Grant Books (London)
5th & 6th Floors
52–54 Southwark Street
London SE1 1UN

hardiegrantbooks.com

A Cataloguing-in-Publication entry is available from
the catalogue of the National Library of Australia
at www.nla.gov.au

Sticky Fingers, Green Thumb
ISBN 978 1 74379 346 6

Publishing Director: Jane Willson
Managing Editor: Marg Bowman
Project Editor: Loran McDougall
Editor: Simon Davis
Design Manager / Designer: Jessica Lowe
Typesetter: Patrick Cannon
Illustrator: Yan Yan Candy Ng
Photographers: Tara Pearce, Tim Hillier
Stylist: Brigid Wald
Home Economist: Lindsay Harris
Production Manager: Todd Rechner
Production Coordinator: Tessa Spring

Colour reproduction by
Splitting Image Colour Studio

Printed in China by
1010 Printing International Limited

If you are using wildflowers or foraged herbs, always check
a reputable source to ensure that the plants you are using
are non-toxic, organic and unsprayed. Hardie Grant Books
cannot be held responsible for any adverse reactions.